*"Will You Answer, 'The Call' Or
Sit On The Sidelines?"*

Chosen

"Now What"

By

Michele Valerie

ISBN: 978-1-953194-08-4

ISBN 978-1-953194-87-9

Table of Contents

ACKNOWLEDGMENTS

1 Would like to acknowledge my loving parents. An abundant blessing to family and friends.

To my faithful sister in the Lord, thank you for seeing the best in me and honoring the assignment upon my life to birth this divine book from the Lord Himself and for writing the forward by being obedient to God.

A special thanks to the publishers and staff at Believe In Your Book Publishing, along with Photographer Will Miller (www.willmillerphoto.com) who helped support and see this vision and mandate come to pass. Thank you!

DEDICATIONS

To my Heavenly Father "Abba"—

Who has brought me through a mighty long way, I love you.

To my Lord and Savior Jesus Christ "Yeshua" —

I love you with all my heart.

To my priceless Holy Spirit —.

My faithful friend and companion I love you.

FOREWORD

I have personally seen the walk that Michele walks, and I have personally seen her transformation process take place before my very eyes... like a caterpillar wrapped within its cocoon and suddenly let out into a beautiful, astonishing butterfly. Michele is someone that if you ever get a chance to experience her in person, you will not want to leave her presence. She is a carrier of the purest joy and always carries a smile that lights up any room.

I have been profoundly inspired by seeing her transformation from feeling ignored and feeling unselected by man to knowing without a doubt that she is "Chosen" by the Most High God! I have witnessed her feelings of powerlessness, where she mustered up all her strength, taking all her pain to turn it into her power to move forward... which has resulted in her becoming the powerhouse she is today. Her ability to love and care deeply, her loyalty level as a person, and her great devotion to Jesus is simply refreshing.

It is an honor to write a forward to this heartfelt and life changing book. I am so proud to call Michele one of my close's friends. I am thankful to God that He has allowed our paths to cross, and for our hearts to connect. The privilege of having her as a friend has changed my life for the better!

Be inspired as Michele Valerie takes you by the hand and walks you through this transformation process of being hand selected by God as His Chosen Vessel. If you will embrace this book with a mindset that is ready for true inner change, then get ready. by the time you are done reading this, you will not recognize yourself!

~ Evangelist Carla D Monroe

CHOSEN

By:
Michele Valerie

There is a Chosen call on your life
That only you can answer.

        There is a Chosen journey for your life
           That only you can take.

There is a Chosen moment in your life
That only you can experience.

        There is a Chosen song in your life
           That only you can sing.

There is a Chosen People for your life
That only you can lead.

        There is a Chosen vision for your life
           That only you can fulfill.

There is a Chosen eternal home in heaven for you
That only you can accept freely.

MY CHOSEN TESTIMONY

By:
Michele Valerie

I'm what most people would call a PK's kid (A Pastor Kid). The enemy came to me at a young age to tell me lies about God's unfailing love for me. It was done through negative words and actions that I experience multiple times, from those far or close to me. I personally know what it is like to have gone through times of loneliness, being homeless, depleted, rejected, abandoned and completely hopeless. Yet, through it all, I can stand up today and still say that I'm not ashamed of the Gospel of Jesus Christ; for it is the power for which all men must be saved (Romans 1 vs. 1-17.)

As an encourager, a birther and exhorter, one might conclude that I have led a life free of warfare. Truthfully my story be told, the only reason that I'm alive today is because of (Jeremiah 29:11 & Joshua 1:8-9). The word of God reminded me that God's plan was to prosper me and give me an expected end. His command was that I was to be strong and courageous, to stand and confess the word of God daily, and to remind myself that He came and that I may have life, and life more abundantly (John 10:10). It is my passion and desire to see God's people fulfill the call, purpose and the destiny of God in their lives, and to usher the Bride of Christ to see themselves as God sees them. Help them to become fully aware that they are truly, fearfully and wonderfully made in the image of God and to come into the truth that they are exactly who God says they are in every area of their lives. My heart felt and continuous cry (Psalms 133) Is my call, purpose and commission from the Lord, that we the Bride of Christ will come into the unity of our Lord and Savior Jesus Christ.

~Prayer of repentance~

I acknowledge with my mouth and heart that Jesus Christ is my Lord and Savior. I confess that I am a sinner, and I ask for Your forgiveness. I believe You died for my sins and rose from the dead. I turn from my sins and invite You to come into my heart and life.

CHAPTER-1
THE REJECTION TRUTH

To be acquainted with rejection is one of the worst feelings anyone can go through. Rejection does not discriminate. It can begin as early as in the womb and as late as ninety-two years old and up. However, precious Chosen one, please know that there are healthy and unhealthy types of rejection. I don't know if you have ever experienced any form of rejection by your peers, a loved one, a friend, your co-worker, your employer, or even from a complete stranger. Maybe you have learned the art of rejecting yourself because you have been told all of your life you were useless, and to go ahead and just die already. Wow, you mean to tell me that the world and even those closest to you can be so cruel? Yes, God's Chosen vessel, you are living in a generation where the Bible speaks of people who will become lovers of themselves and will not care about the well-being of their fellowmen.

There is a familiar passage in the bible that describes what being rejected from the womb looks like. In Ezekiel 16:3-6

KJV, "And say, Thus saith the Lord GOD unto Jerusalem; Thy birth and thy nativity is of the land of Canaan; thy father was an Amorite, and thy mother a Hittite. And as for thy nativity, on the day thou wast born thy navel was not cut, neither wast thou washed in water to supple thee; thou wast not salted at all, nor swaddled at all. None eye pitied thee, to do any of these unto thee, to have compassion upon thee; but thou wast cast out in the open land, to the lothing of thy person, on the day that thou wast born. And when I passed by thee, and saw thee polluted in thine own blood, I said unto thee when thou wast in thy blood, Live; yea, I said unto thee when thou wast in thy blood, Live." God is using this metaphor with His beloved Israel to demonstrate to us how much He cared enough to rescue His people when their own parents had rejected them. Israel, as you know, were not supposed to intermingle with other cultures according to God's commandments, they were to stay within their culture and become a fruitful and God-fearing people and nation. However, God's Chosen people did not fully obey the voice of the Lord, lingered and interacted with the other cultures who were around them, only to find themselves rejected, used and abused after the other cultures were done with them.

Have you ever given so much of yourself to something, or someone, knowing that you were not in the perfect will of God? Instead, you were trying to please two masters because you believed that you could make everything work as you have always done before. Now you find yourself in a dilemma between choosing God's voice or your own voice that tells you like the serpent in the Garden of Eden; God did not say those exact words and you would not surely die. Do well to remember that the enemy of your soul is a master manipulator; he will stop at nothing to see you destroy and forfeit the call of God on your life and He will go to any extent, to see to it, that you are completely defenseless. He will turn you against yourself, against your loved ones, against your close associates, and most of all, the ultimate goal of the enemy of your soul is to turn you against your Heavenly Father's voice and His will for your life. The rejection key is what he will use to gain access to your innermost being.

He will play on your vulnerabilities in more ways than you can imagine. Furthermore, He will keep you distracted and unfocused on who you truly are in the eyes of your Heavenly Father. The rejection factor is a constant manipulation by the enemy of your soul in order to control your thoughts and decisions and to make you weak in your own power. I want you to know that nothing you can do in this raging war that you have found yourself in, will be able to get you out even if you try by your own capabilities or by your own strength. It will only be by God's abilities and power that will ultimately bring you out of this war in this place of complete darkness, and into His marvelous and glorious light intended for you all along. There is where you will come to rise and shine like never before.

In Philippians 4:13 KJV, "I can do all things through Christ who strengthens me." Thank God for this powerful, life changing and comforting scripture. It reassures me that it is really never in my own strength, but in God I find my identity, because when I am weak, my Heavenly Father is strong. Knowing that, I am able to walk freely with peace due to such marvelous revelation. Have you ever felt so defeated and weary that you wouldn't make it to see another day because your adversary is convincing you that you are not strong enough, and that God doesn't care about you or the desires of your heart? He is determined to make sure you do not get the revelation that God is, in every way, concerned about you and what you are going through right now.

Maybe you have just been rejected from the one who promised that they would always be there, through the good and the bad times. Now, you find yourself lying on a cold floor for endless days unable to do the simplest tasks, like basic hygiene skills. You are numb and cannot move or feel anything. Maybe, you just received a blow from one of your children when they said that they no longer need your assistance in their lives. They have chosen their friends and acquaintances to guide them instead of the wisdom and love that you have poured into them over the years, and now your heart is breaking beyond repair. You may have rejected yourself time after time because the very people who should have nurtured you are the same people that broke you down to make you believe you were nothing and have nothing to offer. They made you believe that their lives would be easier if you just disappeared. Unknown to them, all you truly want to do is just die and be out of your misery.

You are not alone in any of these instances. I, too, know the sting of being rejected from loved ones. Rejected from those I thought were my closest friends, associates, peers, employers and coworkers, even complete strangers. Sometimes, I felt rejected by my Heavenly Father Himself, and most of all, I felt the rejection toward myself. I would like to take the time to share some of my personal stories with you. Perhaps you will see that in your own Chosen journey, the road toward the will and call of God upon your life is not one that you have to go through on your own. We all have a God-given Chosen journey, and it will not always be a bed of roses, but your heavenly Father has promised to be there with you every step of the way even when you do not feel Him there. In the darkest hour of your life is when you must remember God's promises and visions which He has made to you. When the midnight hour comes, you do not faint, but you are able to stand on every one of His precious words which He has spoken over your life. Because when you come out, His word will surely bring it all to pass as we read in Isaiah 55:11-13 KJV, "So shall my word be that goeth forth out of my mouth: it shall not return unto me void, but it shall accomplish that which I please, and it shall prosper in the thing whereto I sent it. For ye shall go out with joy and be led forth with peace; the mountains and the hills shall break forth before you into singing, and all the trees of the fields shall clap their hands. Instead of the thorn shall come up the tree, and instead of the brier shall come up the myrtle tree: and it shall be to the LORD for a name, for an everlasting sign that shall not be cut off." You must know if God said it, that He will do it. When He has spoken over your life, the lives of your loved ones, to your ministry, to your business, and to your dream; to anything that He has placed on the inside of you, it shall come to pass. As sure as it has been decreed it will surely be established. Taking this bold step to share my own Chosen rejection experience with you would not have been possible if my wonderful counselor and comforter, the Holy Spirit, had not inspired me to write this priceless and anointed, life transforming book. I will begin by sharing the revelation the Lord gave me when I was having a hard time accepting myself because I felt that I was not good enough. Not just in my own eyes, the eyes of others and not to mention, in the eyes of my Heavenly Father.

Before I begin, let me make this extremely clear: I love my mother very much— no matter what I may have gone through or experienced, temporarily during my childhood or adolescent years. My heart never permitted me to forget the amazing woman my beautiful Mother was and still is. Her volume of love and compassion for her family and others spoke even more loudly as I grew older, it was truly impeccable. I will forever carry her in my heart, and I will always rise up and call her blessed. I love you, Mom. Furthermore, this dedication of my love goes to both of my parents.

What a despicable place to be when you feel you are not even valued to the one who has created you and calls you fearfully and wonderfully made. I will begin by sharing the revelation as to when the stages of rejection started in my life. The Lord revealed to me, like the story we read earlier in Book of Ezekiel Chapter 16: 3-6. It all began in the womb for me. When the doctors told my mom she was expecting twins, this news came as a big surprise to her. Anyone could feel the joy and excitement in the air since it would be her first time being a mother. However, a little less than a year after the twins were born, I was making my grand entrance into the world. Unknown to me, my presence would not be celebrated as the arrival of my brother and sister had been. I must give you a brief history of my mother's life to help bring clarity to why she did not intentionally mean to reject me from the womb, but it was out of her own pain and frustration. Her father died when she was only two years old. In order to take care and to support my mother and her two younger siblings, my grandmother went to work early and came home late to provide for her family. Essentially leaving my mother to become the primary caregiver to her siblings. Needless to say, it wasn't my mothers plan as an adult to continue to take care of twins and then the arrival of an unexpected third child less than a year apart.

I can imagine the burden that must have been on her as a young mother. However, it did not erase the pain and rejection that came to me while I was still in the womb. I thank God that my mother did not decide to have an abortion. As grateful as I am, the sting of rejection still affected me as I spent nine months in the belly of my mother, who did not carry joy in her heart but regret and disappointment that I was arriving so soon after she Just recently gave birth to twins. I can only speak of the role that I began to play in the family due to the rejection that had been imposed on me while in the womb, I was the loving child always trying to keep the peace at any cost. I was bubbly and happy, I just wanted to bring much joy and laughter along with peace in my atmosphere even as a young innocent child. I would not stop until I could bring a smile to your face. All the while, even at a young age, I was rejecting and covering my own hurt and need for much nurturing because I was being overlooked for the adorable twins.

I gave and gave from my own little empty love tank until I began to lose my own identity of who I was. I was a loving child but inside I kept looking for someone to give back to me. I had no balance in my life and I did not know the damage I was doing to myself by giving away all of my love and affection with no reciprocation. All I would try to do was to make everyone around me happy so that I did not have to be the burden that I constantly felt that I was, nor the unfortunate accident that should never have happened.

I can truly say that no child should bear such burden, especially one of being rejected from the womb. I can remember going to school trying to find love and acceptance through my friends by giving them my things that I liked and being nice so everyone could like me. I had no idea who I was— who my true self was. I was on a search to find love and the only way I knew how, in my young mind, was through the giving of myself. Even if that meant giving from an empty love tank. Over time, I carried that into my adult life. I can only thank God, for His grace, that my parents became believers when I was a young girl and began providing me with a stable foundation in the Lord. This introduced me to the fear of the Lord and allowed me to also stay grounded in the word of God daily. By God's grace and mercy, I did not go around selling or giving my body away even though I was still searching for the love I did not receive during my childhood or in my adolescent years.

I began to throw what little love I had left to my church family and friends, in order to fill the void that I felt from not receiving it at home. How many of you know that when you have a depleted love tank, there is nothing in this world that can fill that void like your Heavenly Father? Only when you have exhausted all your resources, when you have slowed down and shut out all of the noise, please know that you can actually hear the soft tender voice of your Heavenly Father calling you. It is then that you realize everything, and everyone has wrongfully let you down to the point that you do not have enough strength, faith or love left. It becomes hard to believe that God can be different from all those people you trusted to give that same genuine love, as you have so freely given. No matter how hard you wished or how long you waited, they never kept the promise to reciprocate that genuine love back to you. I was so tired of the empty promises that the last thing I needed to hear was to give my heart to a God who claimed that He would keep His word. That He would not forsake nor abandon me like so many others had. My heart could not take another stab. I had nothing left to give and I did not trust that God had anything left to give me. Everyone else was always taking from me. "What was going to be different with God," I thought in my infinite mind. You see precious Chosen one, my relationship with God was based on what I heard, or read, about Him in the bible. At the time, I did not have a personal relationship with Him. I could not fathom Him as someone who would love me unconditionally and not want anything back in return. You see the people in my life, or those that I dealt with, were always either taking from me or pretending to care about me but when the road met the rubber they were nowhere to be found.

It was hard for me to come to terms with knowing that I had a Heavenly Father who saw true authentic beauty in me. When all of my life I was compared, criticized and judged. The message that was being sent to me as a young adult was that I was not good enough, I never did anything right and somehow God had messed up when He created me. I felt like I was sent here to just deal with the defects of who I was, based on the view of those who should have had my best interest in mind. What a horrible place to find yourself when you have been so distraught and beaten down verbally and emotionally. There was nothing that anyone could say to help me build back a place of security. They often say hurt people, hurt people. When I looked in the mirror, all I saw was a reaction of someone who is not good enough. Yet, when I was constantly being looked down by others because of their own personal struggles and their own insecurities, which lead them to their own suffering from their own self-hatred and abuse, I now became the victim and personal target of their own hurt and frustration as well.

I remember on one particular day walking home on the last day of school, before summer break. There was a bridge where the other children would walk across, and they would be looking down at me. There was a particular group of gothic kids who always wore black, and it was utterly

19

depressing to look upon them. There was this one young boy among them, he was in a wheelchair blurting out derogatory comments about the color of my skin. They were Caucasian and I remember looking up and actually feeling sorry for the whole group. Out of nowhere, he leaned over the rail and spit down and barely missed my hand. As the other ones in the group kept laughing. I got home that day and took a shower to just wash the care of that day from me and just cried. I asked the Lord, in my young and innocent heart, what did I do wrong and where was He to allow this to happen to me? This incident confirmed more of what I thought all along, there was nothing good in me worth loving.

I eventually made it through my high school years as a very shy and withdrawn young adult, who was always running straight home after school. Because of my low self-esteem and a life filled with little or no positive affirmations growing up, I did not join any sports although I desired too. To me, all the other girls appeared to look better or played better than me. I felt like I had nothing to offer so I would run home, sit in front of the television and escape my reality even if it was just for a few hours everyday. My parents were hardly home at that time, so we learned to fend for ourselves and that meant eating whatever was available to eat at the time whether it was healthy or not. Needless to say, health was not a number one concern in my household. The idea of eating together was rare and was only on holidays such as Thanksgiving, Christmas and special occasions like birthdays. My lack of knowledge and understanding of good nutrition had taken a toll and the result led to negative eating habits and a negative image of myself. Which in turn, added more insecurity, making me not feel pretty enough. My earthly father, whom I loved dearly with all my heart, and I knew he loved me too, but he could not see my inner brokenness and negative self image battle I was going through every single day of my existence. He thought I did not want to be healthy, when the truth be told I just needed to know I was loved and accepted where I was and that I did have the strength to change my circumstances and that I too deserve to be happy and healthy, because that reality and truth for me seem so far beyond my reach due to the broken state that I was trapped in. But the other downfall as a growing young lady, when you have a mother who is constantly working and was hardly home, you are left to figure out things for yourself, as to what the life of a teenage girl should be and having no one to help you go through the changes of being a young adolescent . As the days and years went by, I learned to make do with the limited knowledge that I had. I did not trust a lot of people, so I had no one to go to for the help I needed, as I came into my adolescence.

To be rejected in the womb by the person who should be there for you the most, your mother, yet she is more consumed with work and life than dealing with the responsibility of taking care of her child, it was extremely disheartening. She assumed that I was old enough to take care of myself. I remember one incident, when my older sister had started her cycle as a young girl. I recall I was passing by the room and overheard my mother talking to her. She was talking to her about the changes that were happening to her body with a tender motherly voice as she took the time out to deal with the issue at hand with my older sister. The minute my mother noticed that I was by the door, she looked at me and told me to go away and stay out of grown folks business. I don't need to tell you how very little and rejected I felt at that moment. Ironically, a month later I got my cycle and tried to tell my mother about it, but she told me to stop exaggerating and to go and sit down. Well, needless to say that right there the relationship between my mother and I was not always built on a solid foundation after that night. That incident closed the door of trust and opened communication between the two of us. I love my mother with all my heart but what I needed was comfort, nurturing and acceptance, similar to what she gave to my older siblings. Instead, I felt like I had to fight to earn her love and acceptance. My heart broke that day.

Even still, with all that I had been through, I managed to muster up the courage to hold my head up and say to myself, "I matter. I am worthy." Even if I was unsure of my path, I knew that to someone, or something— I was worthy. It was only by God's grace that I did not go sleeping around in search of the missing piece to the puzzle; in search of an answer as to why I was rejected by my loved ones, my peers and my friends and most importantly, the reason why I could not accept that God loved me. I suppose it was because I was constantly reminded and told that I was unlovable. It felt as though something was missing in me and that I was just not good enough to believe that God would care about me, just the way I was.

I did not know what true love was. I wanted to know but no one had taken the time out to show me. I learned to shut down my emotions and put up my guard. I built an invisible wall that I did not realize was there. Let me ask you a vital question, God's Chosen one, do you know what it is like to hurt so bad until you can't feel anything but numbness all around you? You don't want to be anyone else no matter how rejected others have made you feel, all you really want is to be accepted and loved as your true, authentic self. God's precious Chosen one, I know that the bruises and the scars are still there. Although the healing of the outward part has taken place, the inner part still cries out to be heard and to be set free from the old stigma that has been placed on you. In my heart of hearts, I know that the walls and barriers that I put up were so that I would not cross over and hurt anyone. In retrospect, those same walls and barriers blocked myself from receiving authentic love from anyone who was willing to truly extend themselves to me.

How could I trust that anyone truly had my best interest in mind when all I have known was the hurt and the pain of one rejection after another? Precious Chosen one, I could not learn to love and accept myself let alone receive God's love for me. I felt like a huge disappointment and wondered when this nightmare would stop. I cried to God on many occasions, begging to go home to Heaven and be with Him. His response was always no. I started to get so mad at God for the constant 'no' in my infinite mind, that I wanted Him to just disown me like everyone else had. I wanted Him to give up on me and let me be. All God kept telling me was that I would live to be very old, and He would take excellent care of me. Now how many of you know, when you are in a rejected and depressive state of wanting to be raptured, the last thing you want to hear is that you are going to grow old gracefully. Then, He proceeded to tell me that I have a group of people whom He has called me to and has assigned to me, and the fact that I wanted to forfeit and abort my destiny and let these people perish was unacceptable. I wish I could say that I said, "Lord, I am sorry. Please forgive me, I repent." Instead, I just looked over at a young woman that was next to me and in my heart, I told God she looks like she would fit the profile for the very call He had for my life so why can't He just send her.

I don't need to tell you, but that did not go well at all. When God gets quiet, He gets quiet because His intentions for you are final and He will not change his mind on your destiny. I am writing this book that He has mandated me to share with you, dear Chosen one. Believe me, I was far from overjoyed that my Heavenly Father was requiring me to stay a day longer in this mean, cruel, unfair and unjust world. I felt He was being just as cruel by asking me to stay on this earth. Especially, when all I really wanted was to be in His loving and tender arms, where I could be safe and away from the constant reminder of all the rejection. It is easy to fall prey to the opinions of other people and to the lies from the enemy of the soul. It is even easier when this kind of abuse begins at a young age and destroys your very identity. I believed those lies and opinions. I believed that I was what they said I was, instead of who God said I am. The enemy of the soul knowingly comes to drive a wedge between you and your Heavenly Father.

This is a battle you cannot fight nor win on your own. You will need the grace and faith of God to know that He does truly have a destiny and a divine will for your life. The Bible declares in Proverbs 19:21 KJV, " There are many devices in a man's heart; nevertheless the counsel of the LORD, that shall stand." What a scripture to describe the character of God! It is not the plans that you have for your own life that will take precedence if you are truly one of God's "Chosen" vessels; it is God's plan for your life that will prosper no matter how many different paths you try to take. What is most phenomenal about your God-given Chosen journey is that even when you feel like you are in a rejected state, God continues to bring you comfort. He is not rejecting you in an unhealthy way nor is He trying to make you feel negative about yourself. Rather, he is reminding you that the plans you are trying to orchestrate without His approval, are not for you. I have been there when God, Himself, brought me through His own healthy rejection process. It was a time when I was struggling the most. While that rejection process is real and trying, believe that He can get you to the place where you can humbly dwell in His presence and anointing. When you understand that not all rejection is unhealthy, you are opening doors for blessings in disguise.

God's healthy rejection process is called death to self, and I will gladly explain it to you. Whenever God wants to get a point across, He will require that you have lived or walked out the very process that He is calling you to fulfill. Sometimes that process brings rejection to the very things you want and desire, so that God may be Glorified. Whether it be a relationship, desire dreams or just a heart desire that you have not seen come to pass or you have chosen to put whatever that thing that means a lot to you before God and everything and anyone else. You have taken the road that is traveled more because you did not want to sacrifice or be obedient to God or the will of God Chosen One. I will tell you that nothing you can desire in this life can replace the sovereign perfect will of God for your life. Because it was in my desperation of wanting to hold on to whatever felt or looked like love and the enemy will have you think that you need to compromise in order to really obtain all that God has for your life. I want to remind you, the chosen one, that the enemy is and will continue to be the father of lies, there is no truth found in him. So therefore, if he is telling you something that is opposite of the will of God for your life, please rest assured that God is not a man who needs to lie or tell you stories to make you feel better. He is God over your life all by Himself, so if you really want to see the move of God's promise come into your life, please stop pursuing your own agenda and pick up God's plan and assignment and His will for your life. Give up your will for God's sovereign perfect will and you will never be disappointed or be let down as long as you take hold unto the hands of an everlasting unchanging hands. Regardless of your past, your bad decisions or mistakes, God is the one who can clean you up and give you a brand-new beginning from whatever or whoever thought you would always be in this place of desolation and disappointment all the days of your life. No longer will you need to compromise or be in a constant battle over your mind or destiny because His precious Chosen One God has called you to be free to be all that He is calling you to be.

I must be clear, although you know that God will prevent some chapters from being part of your life so you can come into His good and sovereign perfect will for you. There are some experiences that you go through and you may blame yourself, once again, you may find yourself weak and not standing your ground and allowing individuals into your life knowing those you are surrounding yourself with they do not honor God in their own personal lives or in their various relationships with others. Because of your attachment to those individuals, you may then begin to experience such guilt of not being valued by them because they are only able to give you their own version of love and acceptance from their own empty and depleted tank. The hurt and shame of what happened to you may have lasted for a long time but determined that you would not be hurt like this ever again. So, you placed a wall between you and anyone who tried to come towards your heart. You may once again find yourself not having anything left to give. You feel depleted, devastated and most of all you do not want to feel anything, concerning anyone. This situation of your Chosen journey may change the paths to one where you began to merely exist without any desire to live. God is possibly teaching you a very valuable lesson that you may not be quite ready for. He took me to His word in Isaiah 54: 4-10 KJV, "Do not be afraid; you will not suffer shame. Do not fear disgrace; you will not be humiliated. You will forget the shame of your youth and remember no more the reproach of your widowhood. For your Maker is your husband the Lord Almighty is his name the Holy One of Israel is your Redeemer; he is called the God of all the earth."

"The Lord will call you back as if you were a wife deserted and distressed in spirit— a wife who married young, only to be rejected, says your God. For a brief moment I abandoned you, but with deep compassion I will bring you back. In a surge of anger, I hid my face from you for a moment, but with everlasting kindness I will have compassion on you, says the Lord your Redeemer. To me this is like the days of Noah, when I swore that the waters of Noah would never again cover the earth. So now I have sworn not to be angry with you, never to rebuke you again. Though the mountains be shaken, and the hills be removed, yet my unfailing love for you will not be shaken nor my covenant of peace be removed, says the Lord, who has compassion on you." Be very certain and clear that there is nothing God is going to require of you, in your journey, that is not confirmed through His word. Of course, you will have to tough it out just like His Chosen servants had to do in the Bible. For me, I realized that God was not angry to the point where He was rejecting me to intentionally harm me. He was letting me know that my behavior and disobedience to His will and purpose for my life were being jeopardized through the lifestyle I was living in. I was trying to please both people and God, when the bible clearly states one cannot serve two masters. He will love one more and hate the other.

Ultimately, God took me on my very own Chosen journey of what I would eventually call "God's healthy rejection." This journey was imperative if I wanted a real and true relationship with God. This meant that there were times in this journey when my closest friends could not help me, I had to walk out my own personal chosen journey all by myself. I had to unlearn my old ways of being and doing and start accepting the process of rejecting my old ways. These old ways were mostly my dependency on trying to find love from people and things. I had to learn how to trust and fall in love with my Husband and my Maker, Jesus the true lover of my soul. God led me like His Chosen servant, Abraham, in Genesis 12:1-4 KJV, "Now the Lord had said unto Abram, Get thee out of thy country, and from thy kindred, and from thy father's house, unto a land that I will shew thee: And I will make of thee a great nation, and I will bless thee, and make thy name great; and thou shalt be a blessing: And I will bless them that bless thee, and curse him that curseth thee: and in thee shall all families of the earth be blessed. So, Abram departed, as the Lord had spoken unto him; and Lot went with him: and Abram was seventy and five years old when he departed out of Haran." God will tell you the promise but in your Chosen journey there is a whole process that you will know nothing of— just trust God at His word. However, I want you to know that as you

31

go forth, you will start to realize there is an unexpected middle portion between the process and the promise that God had failed to discuss with you.

God knows the end from the beginning. He does not forget the intricate parts of your journey. He is just wise enough to know how much He can tell you and, certainly, how much you can handle. What a gracious, merciful and gracious Heavenly Father that we have. Part of the healthy rejection process is learning not to lean on yourself or others that God wants to completely remove from your life. This is to help you become all that He has purpose in His heart and plan for you. I have learned that no one or anything can stop your God Chosen journey. Only your disobedience to the voice and will of God and the hardening of your heart to His Chosen call upon your life. No, the process to the promise is not articulated in step by step instructions; however, God tells us in His word Romans 8:35-39 KJV, "Who shall separate us from the love of Christ? Shall trouble or hardship or persecution or famine or nakedness or danger or sword?" As it is written: "For your sake we face death all day long; we are considered as sheep to be slaughtered."

"Know, in all these things we are more than conquerors through Him who loved us. For I am convinced that neither death nor life, neither angels nor demons, neither the present nor the future, nor any powers, neither height nor depth, nor anything else in all creation, will be able to separate us from the love of God that is in Christ Jesus our Lord." What a powerful truth! There is absolutely no guide in the process to the promise. Regardless of how difficult it seems at the time, it will not separate God's love for His Chosen vessel. I can truly say this passage has helped me to realize all of my stages of rejection, that I have previously discussed. From the infancy stage of rejection, up until my adulthood, one thing has remained faithful and stable in my life — God's unconditional love for me. Even though my mind could not comprehend why God loved me, my Heavenly Father continued to see the best in me until I could receive and believe that He truly had my best intentions in mind. God was not out trying to hurt me or put another unhealthy rejection label on me, He truly did care for me. When I went through the steps from my process to my promise, it was made known to me that I was rejecting the old mindset of all the unhealthy labels that had been placed on me. God was removing them, but He has His own way of doing things. While I may not have understood it at the time, I knew His loving and tender arms meant me no harm.

Like God's Chosen servant Abraham, when he left his home and family and sojourned to a strange land without knowing what his journey would entail; he chose to have faith and trust in His Heavenly Father. Similarly, I had to do the same. If you are in the beginning of your God Chosen journey, or are being summoned by your Heavenly Father, answer the call. Say 'yes' with a sincere and authentic heart. You may find that your God Chosen process may lead you to real and authentic experiences and circumstances, knowing that God will make the provision as He orders your footstep.

The process of surrendering to God is rough! It is not for the faint of heart or weak in mind. There are times when you will find yourself crying and screaming out to God for the process to stop because the pain is too much to bear. In return, all you may get is silence. Just know that God is continuing to silently lead you to your destiny, but you do have to surrender your own self will to His will and ultimate plan for your life. The journey is difficult and may not quite be what you thought you signed up for, but it is all worth it.

I can remember sitting in my car and telling God that I could run home to safety and forget this whole assignment and Chosen journey that He wanted to take me through. But I was wise enough to know that if I did not surrender to him now, I would have to surrender to him sooner or later. I wisely decided that the point of surrender would come, and I could make it easier by saying yes instead of fighting it. I could learn to reject the voice of the enemy of my soul, who would love nothing more than to see me stuck in a state of rejection and depletion, who would love nothing more than to come and steal, kill and destroy my Chosen destiny. So, I said Yes. Let me remind you, you are not reading this anointed and appointed, God-divine orchestrated book by error, He knew you needed to know the truth of what your God Chosen journey would require of you. There will be an authentic 'yes' when you totally surrender to the infallible truth that your Chosen journey will require everything of you. This also means that it will take God's courage and boldness along with every wound, every pain and rejection from your past, to bring you to the point where you can freely say, "I am so totally, completely sold out to God and His Chosen call upon my life." Therefore, no person, devil, imposter, deceiver, impersonator will stop you and cause you to forfeit your God-given Chosen, appointed and anointed destiny. You will finish your race and you will run the race well. Just like God's Chosen Apostle Paul in 2 Timothy 4:7-8 KJV, " I have fought a good fight, I have finished my course, I have kept the faith: Henceforth there is laid up for me a crown of righteousness, which the Lord, the righteous judge, shall give me at that day: and not to me only, but unto all them also that love his appearing."

We each have a race to run and a fight to be fought, don't let anyone belittle you any longer. Forgive yourself of past failures and the rejections of your past, because when you decide to accept and walk toward your God's Chosen call, it will be in the peace and rest of God. When the load becomes too heavy for you to bear, know that because you have said 'yes' to your Heavenly Father that He will certainly help you carry that load. He will help you run the race and fight the fight of Faith that He has called you to fight. There will be days when the fight and the race get intense and hard but you are never alone. You are always at the mercy, grace and favor of your Heavenly Father. He has his angels already aligned to be dispatched concerning you. He has every hair on your head already accounted for and your name is written in the palm of His hand and the greatest joy is that He does all this while He sings and rejoices over you, as He continues to cover you with His Banner of Love.

He is your Chosen king of Kings and Lord of Lords. He has Chosen you to finish your race and assignment, well and strong. So, gird up your loins and put on your full armor because when you answer your God Chosen call, with an authentic and sincere yes, you will see every destiny, dream, vision, promise and all prophetic words come to pass in your life. All those who criticized you so openly, failing to acknowledge that you are God's Chosen, appointed and anointed child, will sit back with their mouth wide open and a genuine heartfelt repentance while God displays you right in front of their faces. Dear Chosen one, always remains humble, meek and submitted always to the Lord. *Let us proceed...*

CHAPTER-2
THE MISUNDERSTOOD TRUTH

Webster defines the word misunderstood as; not appreciated or given sympathetic understanding; a failure to understand or interpret correctly. A disagreement or quarrel. Being misunderstood can leave you feeling frustrated and defeated. We have all been there. Instances of being misunderstood by our friends, family and peers. It is a lonely place to be when your voice is begging to be heard and your heart is vulnerable to judgment and criticism that is being placed upon you. All you want is for someone to take the time to hear you out and try to understand. I have been there. I know how uncomfortable it gets when you are standing and doing all that God has called you to do and you are trying your best every day to stay on point as you answer the call of God in your life and yet no one else sees that.

This is when you begin to get the most opposition from those who should have your back. Some will begin to call you goody two shoes and some will ask you if you think you are God's gift to the world. They don't see all the chaos that hides behind your smile, that you have carried all day. They are prejudging you based on their own lack of contentment, self-control, insecurity and inferiority. Allow no one to come in and take the little piece of joy, love and peace you have managed to muster up while life keeps hitting you from all directions. No one has the right to come and make you feel less than or belittle your condition just because they do not have a disciplined life. They are not intimately walking with God to understand the process and path that God has you on and call He has placed upon your life. You will find more people on your Chosen journey who are quick to remind you of your failures, faults and shortcomings than those who are willing to lift you up and out of your current situation.

Never give anyone or anything the power to feel that they have a right to speak into your life. They do not have the right to speak on what they do not know. If they knew what they were talking about, they would know that no one in their right mind would choose to live under a bridge or eat from the garbage can every day. No one in the right mind would want to stand on the road to beg for food or give their children to the state because they cannot afford to take care of them. Little do they know that some choices you have made in life were no fault of your own. Life handed you a card and all you were trying to do, with the little information and knowledge that you had, was play that card to the best of your ability. Nothing is more heart-breaking than to hear stories of people doing things that are considered a "disgrace" in society because no one took the time, or cared enough to tell them there is an answer to their plight in life and that the road to your journey is not a dead-end track. The Word of God tells us that in John 3:16-18 KJV, "For God so loved the world, that he gave his only begotten Son, that whosoever believeth in him should not perish, but have everlasting life. For God sent not his Son into the world to condemn the world; but that the world through him might be saved. He that believeth on him is not condemned: but he that believeth not is condemned already, because he hath not believed in the name of the only begotten Son of God." It is not just those hurting in the world that are misunderstood. Often, you can find the same people sitting within the four walls of a church being judged because their praise and worship is too loud, too boisterous or because they pray a bit longer. They do not seem to fit the "profile" of what a Chosen child of God should look like. We find such outrageous discrimination not only in the world but in God's very house. God says, in Mark 11:17 KJV, "And he taught, saying unto them, Is it not written,

My house shall be called of all nations the house of prayer? but ye have made it a den of thieves." How dare we pretend that all is well in God's house while there are so many in His house hurting, crying out for the love and compassion of God to come back and reign in His Temple? The church building is not the temple; we as God's Chosen ones, are the temple. When one hurts, we all should hurt.

Yet, we tend to disregard another's pain as insignificant compared to the pain we are going through. We have managed to put people on a "preferred" list, if they do not fit the profile, we do not make time for them. Where is the love and heart of God to a dying church and a dying world? It's time we begin to see people as God sees them. They matter to God, so they should matter to us. God's Chosen vessels are not just numbers to Him, they are the very ones that His only begotten son Jesus gave His life for on the cross. Their life matters and makes a difference in God's house as well as to this lost and dying world. It's time for the judgment toward one another to stop. If you do not understand what God is doing in the life of one of His Chosen vessels, then step to the side and allow God to have His way. Be the prayer warrior that God is calling you to be for that Chosen vessel. God has stated in His word, over and over again, that His ways are not our ways. Each of God's

Chosen vessels have a story that is different and custom fit to their own Chosen journey. No two journeys are alike. We all have to walk out the call and purpose of God upon our lives the way that God intended.

Your Chosen journey is not going to resemble anyone else's, and you should not get caught up in the opinions and thoughts of others. God is the only one who knows the end to your Chosen journey. You are only to submit yourself to the will and hands of God and not allow the enemy of your soul to have a say concerning the will and call of God upon your life. For we read in James 4:7 KJV, "Submit yourselves therefore to God. Resist the devil, and he will flee from you." Our first and only obligation is to first submit to God and His authority over our lives and only then will we have the strength and power over the enemy of our soul. Only then, can we resist him and gain the victory each and every time. Submission is not a word most people welcome, but in order to have victory and triumph over the enemy, you are going to have to learn the art of walking in submission and humility. Foremost, to your Heavenly Father, and then toward your fellow man whether they hold a great or small position in your eyes.

You will not find your identity in any person, place or thing. Understand that you are who God has called you to be. God told His Chosen son Gideon, whose circumstance looked nothing like the words that God was speaking over his life, in Judges 6:11 KJV, "The angel of the LORD came and sat down under the oak in Ophrah that belonged to Joash the Abiezrite, where his son Gideon was threshing wheat in a winepress to keep it from the Midianites." When the angel of the LORD appeared to Gideon, he said, "The LORD is with you, mighty warrior." "But sir," Gideon replied, "if the LORD is with us, why has all this happened to us? Where are all his wonders that our fathers told us about when they said, 'Did not the LORD bring us up out of Egypt?' But now the LORD has abandoned us and put us into the hand of Midian." The LORD turned to him and said, "Go in the strength you have and save Israel out of Midian's hand. Am I not sending you?" "But Lord," Gideon asked, "how can I save Israel? My clan is the weakest in Manasseh, and I am the least in my family." The LORD answered, "I will be with you, and you will strike down all the Midianites together." Gideon was the most misunderstood individual and would not have made the "preferred" list that the world, and most of our churches, have going on now these days.

Gideon was in the wine press trying not to be seen by the enemy who was attacking His beloved land, and God's people. He was minding his own business trying to provide for himself and his family when God had a divine appointment with him on this very day. Gideon was not only misunderstood by others, but he did not understand who he was in Christ. God called him by his position in the kingdom, not by the state and condition of what was going on in the environment he was living in. However, Gideon was about to tell God that He had the wrong guy. He might as well go look in the next wine press fifty miles down the road for this Great Man of Valor that He was looking for. Because of life's labels and misunderstanding of the process that God is taking us through, we often take ourselves out of the race. However, be grateful for a loving and compassionate God who will not give up on us or allow us to remain in the misunderstood state that we or others have been put in. We see too much of this misunderstood what is happening around us, where we leave God out of the equation and make choices based on the outside appearance of man. We disregard whether or not his heart is toward the true authentic things of God. Therefore, we catered and pampered the outside apparels. Forgetting that God focuses on the interior of a person foremost.

God, forgive our ignorance and help us to see what you see and not what we want to see or hear in this hour. Like the rising up of people after your own heart, just like your

Chosen servant David. He was not ashamed of who he was to you, even if it meant being misunderstood and losing people and things that were near and dear to him. God's Chosen one, you matter more to your Heavenly Father than anything in this whole world. Lord, let this again be the cries of the heart of your true sons and daughters in this hour and season, that we do not want to be a generation longing for possessions, but a generation filled with your authentic fire and the true power of your Holy Spirit. Lord, like your Chosen servant Daniel in Daniel 9:3-19 KJV, "So I turned to the Lord God and pleaded with him in prayer and petition, in fasting, and in sackcloth and ashes. I prayed to the LORD my God and confessed: "O Lord, the great and awesome God, who keeps his covenant of love with all who love him and obey his commands, we have sinned and done wrong. We have been wicked and have rebelled; we have turned away from your commands and laws. We have not listened to your servants, the prophets, who spoke in your name to our kings, our princes and our fathers, and to all the people of the land. Lord, you are righteous, but this day we are covered with shame—the men of Judah and people of Jerusalem and all Israel, both near and far, in all the countries where you have scattered us because of our unfaithfulness to you. O Lord, we and our kings, our princes and our fathers are covered with shame because we have sinned against you. The Lord our God is merciful and forgiving, even though we have rebelled against him; we have not obeyed the LORD our God or kept the laws he gave us through his servants the prophets. All Israel has transgressed your law and turned away, refusing to obey you. Therefore, the curses and sworn judgments written in the Law of Moses, the servant of God, have been poured out on us, because we have sinned against you. You have filled the words spoken against us and against our rulers by bringing upon us great disaster. Under the whole heaven nothing has ever been done like what has been done to Jerusalem. Just as it is written in the Law of Moses, all this disaster has come upon us, yet we have not sought the favor of the Lord our God by turning from our sins and giving attention to your truth. The Lord did not hesitate to bring the disaster upon us, for the Lord our God is righteous in everything he does; yet we have not obeyed him. Now, O Lord our God, who brought your people out of Egypt with a mighty hand and who made for yourself a name that endures to this day, we have sinned, we have done wrong.

O Lord, in keeping with all your righteous acts, turn away your anger and your wrath from Jerusalem, your city, your holy hill. Our sins and the iniquities of our fathers have made Jerusalem and your people an object of scorn to all those around us. Now, our God, hear the prayers and petitions of your servant. For your sake, O Lord, look with favor on your desolate sanctuary. Give ear, O God, and hear; open your eyes and see the desolation of the city that bears your Name. We do not make requests of you because we are righteous, but because of your great mercy. O Lord, listen! O Lord, forgive! O Lord, hear and act! For your sake, O my God, do not delay, because your city and your people bear your Name. Like Daniel, we too, must come asking for true repentance not just for ourselves but for our entire nation and family, community, city, lost ones, and everyone who has been misunderstood. Heavenly Father, just like your servant Daniel, we ask not for our sake, for we are a shameful and self-seeking and perverse generation who needs to be cleansed, purged and washed under the blood of the Lamb daily. We are asking to be a Holy generation who will truly love you with all of our hearts, might and body and souls. Lord, we ask this petition and request of you for your Holy and Precious name sake.

We don't want to move forward or do anything apart from you. We need your wisdom and guidance to help us be free of the things, the people and from the enemy of our soul that would try to hold us back from ever fulfilling our God's Chosen purpose plan and destiny for our lives. Lord, for you, we want to live and die. We are tired of living a life less than you have orchestrated and provided for us.

Have you been misunderstood by others who should be there for you to pray with you, give you a word of encouragement or just sit in the silent hours with you? In the word of God, Paul and Silas found a praise song in the midnight hour to pull them through. When you look and reach out for love and understanding, all you found was constant criticism because those close to you misunderstood the process which God was taking you through. What have you been going through? Do you struggle to articulate the process, trial and test which God was using in your life to build His character in you, so that you can shine and be filled with His love and Glory? So you can help the very ones who have spoken against your process and bring them to His light and to a lost, hurting and dying world.

Your Chosen journey is not one that people can see with their own two eyes to understand what God is doing in you supernaturally. They will have their own thoughts and opinions, they may criticize or make fun, and some may try to convince you that this "God-thing" is not working but they are wrong. You will be greatly misunderstood for the sake of God's Chosen call upon your life. You must make up your mind like the Apostle Paul states in 1 Corinthians

4:9-13 KJV, "For it seems to me that God has put us apostles on display at the end of the procession, like men condemned to die in the arena. We have been made a spectacle to the whole universe, to angels as well as to men. We are fools for Christ, but you are so wise in Christ! We are weak, but you are strong! You are honored, we are dishonored! To this very hour we go hungry and thirsty, we are in rags, we are brutally treated, we are homeless. We work hard with our own hands. When we are cursed, we bless; when we are persecuted, we endure it; when we are slandered, we answer kindly. Up to this moment we have become the scum of the earth, the refuse of the world." Like the apostle Paul, you too, must stand firm, stand your ground and not be moved through all of the misunderstanding that will come your way.

God has Chosen you for a divine purpose and assignment that will not always look glamorous or inviting or be understood by others. Consider yourself as coal in the process of becoming God's Chosen diamond. The process is nothing welcoming or desiring but if you allow Him to take you through it, you will be amazed and those same people who judged and doubted you, will be as well. So, keep moving and pressing forward, as surely as God has said it concerning you, He will bring every one of His promises to pass in your life. Don't be afraid to be misunderstood by people so that you can gain God's final and divine approval over your life. It is then that you will see the destiny He has for you, and it shall be displayed for all those who have dismissed you from the line up and disqualified you from the race. *Let us proceed...*

CHAPTER-3
THE PAINFUL TRUTH

Here we are in the moment of truth. By now, you have realized that the call of God on your life comes with a cost and it's a very high price to pay. Night after night you've stayed up crying and unable to sleep just because the pain that you are experiencing is far too much for you to articulate. All you want to do is die in the midst of your sorrow. The pain seems like it will never end. Your heart is broken in places you don't even know existed. Your body will not cooperate, all you want is to feel at the time of your greatest distress is numbness but instead the pain magnifies. There is no amount of alcohol or other vices to help ease the pain or fill the void. It feels like someone is repeatedly stabbing at your heart.

Have you ever hurt till you thought there was no possible way to hurt anymore? What has broken your heart so badly that your very own existence has become detestable to you? Where did your heartache begin? Was it at the hands of someone whom you trusted, and they violated your innocence and robbed you of the true pleasure of knowing what real authentic love is? Was it at the church you attended, where you should have received what the true meaning of what God's love looks like, instead you receive your fair share of backstabbing? Was it at the job that you gave your all, only to be passed down for the promotion you have been working so hard for? Was it at the hand of the individual who promised to love you forever, but the time ran out? Was it at the hand of your beloved family who should have treasured you but they, like everyone else, could not see the best in you? Was it at the hand of a deceiver who deceived, used you and left you out in the rain? Who broke your heart? I know you are asking daily, "Why Lord? What did I do?" You have all these questions, but no answer seems to come to mind. You have loved to the best of your abilities; you have given yourself only to have things taken from you. You are depleted, weary and torn and have not received your just reward. The word of the Lord says in Hebrews 11:6 KJV, "But without faith it is impossible to please him: for he that cometh to God must believe that he is, and that he is a rewarder of them that diligently seek him." There were times I often questioned, "Did I miss you my Lord, am I being punished?" I felt like the joke of the town speaking His word, as well as being a witness. Everyone knew that I believed in Him and when they saw my pain, they marked me as a sinner who must have gone astray and is getting what I deserve. I am reminded of God's Chosen servant Job in Job 34: 1-12 KJV, "Furthermore Elihu answered and said, hear my words, O ye wise men; and give ear unto me, ye that have knowledge. For the ear trieth words, as the mouth tasted meat. Let us choose to use judgment: let us know among ourselves what is good. For Job hath said, I am righteous: and God hath taken away my judgment. Should I lie against my right? My wound is incurable without transgression. What man is like Job, who drinks scorn like water? Which goeth in company with the workers of iniquity, and walketh with wicked men? For he hath said, it profiteth a man nothing that he should delight himself with God. Therefore, hearken unto me, ye men of understanding far be it from God, that he should do wickedness; and from the Almighty, that he should commit iniquity.

For the work of a man shall he render unto him and cause every man to find according to his ways', surely God will not do wickedly, nor will the Almighty pervert judgment." He was a Chosen man of God who knew what it was like to lose everything. His children, livelihood, family, friends, you name it, Job lost it. He was pursuing the things of God and doing well to those in his household and to those in his community. What Job did not know was that his story, his process, his pain and his lack of understanding of the process, not only for him but for his friends who spoke so wrongly against his God and his very character, they were speaking out of their infinite knowledge as the scripture above tells us. Job's friends, in their limited human understanding, concluded Job had to have been living a wicked and sinful lifestyle to have all of these calamities come upon him. What other explanation could there be? It all made perfect sense, even Job's wife told him to go ahead and curse God and die. Some people would rather see you die in your situation right now, rather than to speak life to you because they do not understand the way or process God is using you.

You have to stand in the revelation that God is the divine orchestrator, and He will use every pain, process and event in your life. No matter what it looks like in the natural world, God is working fervently behind the scenes to bring the beautiful portrait of your life into its full completion. You will have to cry many nights, you will have to walk many miles, but you will not die full with your chosen purpose and destiny still inside of you. He will pour you out until you are totally empty to where God Himself can come and fill your empty vessel. God does not waste anything. For He said in His own words in Genesis 1: 31 KJV, "And God saw everything that he had made, and behold, it was very good." This revelation of God's word should bring much joy to you, precious Chosen one. No matter what it seems like or feels like, you are not an accident. God has orchestrated every step of your Chosen journey and sometimes the road we have to take may not have been our choice but forced upon us by an individual or life circumstance. It may have been our choice through our lack of ignorance and knowledge.

Whatever the event was that has brought you much pain, know that today you can choose to be better. You don't have to stay in the isolation of your deepest pain. God did not create you to live a life of defeat, filled with pain and turmoil. We are in a war that is raging constantly for our souls, Chosen one, and you must know that God is on your side. He is for you and not against you. The Word of God says in 1 Peter 5:8 KJV, "Be of sober spirit, be on the alert. Your adversary, the devil prowls about like a roaring lion, seeking someone to devour." You see, there is much more at stake than the enemy affecting you with pain to keep you off the course toward your God Chosen destiny. You will win this fight, if you will only believe like a mother that is in labor. The pain is excruciating and unbearable, but it is a process. Part of the process is to acknowledge this pain that you are feeling right now like an indication that the baby is on its way. The same is with your Chosen journey, you have been going through a lot of heartache and pain caused by various situations or individuals that have violated you both in the natural and spirit. Those you should have been able to trust and run too for safety. I do not want you to be ignorant, the word of God clearly tells us how to be successful in our journey in Psalm 118: 8-9 KJV, "It is better to trust in the Lord than to put confidence in man.

It is better to trust in the LORD than to put confidence in princes." We are hurt and devastated when we place our trust in anything other than God. He warns us, with His tender loving and compassionate ways, that only in Him and through Him will we have unspeakable joy, love, and peace. As you set your firm foundation let me help you avoid a lot of heartache in your Chosen journey by placing your eyes on the Lord, and not on an individual or on earthly possessions. When we are willing to face the things that have brought us much pain and learn from them, we can move forward knowing that we have allowed God to heal every wound and areas of our lives that the enemies of our souls have meant to destroy. The word of God in Ecclesiastes 9:11 KJV, "the race is not to the swift, nor the battle to the strong, neither yet bread to the wise, nor yet riches to men of understanding, nor yet favor to men of skill; but time and chance happeneth to them all."

Although the pain and trauma you have experienced thus far did not take place overnight, the scripture above speaks to us to know that there is a process that takes place when God wants to heal you from the pains of yesterday. We have to be willing to acknowledge that the pain happened and be willing to be translucent of what we are feeling. Being naked and unashamed of the life event that happened to you, helps to expose the enemy of your soul from holding you in bondage, as well as it will certainly help make you free. The pain that you are not willing to admit, release and forgive is the very pain that will keep you captive, both you and the person who has done this injustice to you. The act of forgiveness must also be incorporated in the healing process. When we are willing to let go of all the hurt, God can come and fill the broken pieces of our hearts and mend us back together as only He can. Remember, when we are yielded to the person of the Holy Spirit, He will minister to the part of us that we have well-hidden and so numb that we no longer feel anything anymore. Your Heavenly Father specifically says in Psalm 84:11 KJV, "No good thing will He withhold from them that walk uprightly."

What comfort and joy this scripture should bring to your soul! To know that God did not create His Chosen vessel to live a life filled with pain, numbness or hopelessness. We have to know that we have much value in His eyes and what happened to us, however much it was sent by the enemy of our soul, God was and is still on the throne and He is watching over us singing and rejoicing. We must learn, as God's Chosen one, to walk through the pain and the brokenness, admitting that it happened and begin to proclaim your healing. Doing this can also help someone else be set free and to not have to experience the same pain. If they can be delivered from your story, they too, can help someone else come out of the pain they feel is never going to cease. You may have heard the saying when God wants to bless you, He will use a person; and when the enemy wants to mess you up, he will use a person as well. Wow, how can I win this battle and recognize who is for me or against me? God's Chosen servant the Apostle Paul encourages us to ask for the gift of wisdom and the gift of discernment. It would be beneficial for all of us who are willing to not be deceived by the enemy of our soul any longer, if we can willingly come before our Heavenly Father in James 1:5 KJV, "If any of you lack wisdom, let him ask of God, that giveth to all men liberally, and upbraideth not; and it shall be given him."

It is God's desire for you to be well equipped, therefore do not be silent in asking him for much needed wisdom on your Chosen journey. We must pray and ask God to fill us with His precious Holy Spirit, so we can recognize the time and season, and the individuals He would have us connect with. Not everyone will be for you, in your Chosen journey. What may seem like a good thing may not necessarily be the right thing. You must learn to pray to the will of your Heavenly Father for your life. Spend intimate time with Him and become one with Him. You must become one in spirit, body and soul, where He knows all of you and you know all of Him. To be familiar with His voice when He speaks to you in His loving and tender manner. When you make God a priority in your life, the outside circumstances will not affect how you interact with your fellow man and the way they treat you will not be of great importance. The greatest gift you can give yourself is a personal and intimate relationship with God. This will give you great success in your Chosen journey along with spending time in your word will take you to higher heights and deeper depths you have yet to experience with your Heavenly Father.

The pain you have experienced is real and I do not take anything you have gone through lightly. Maybe it has been the betrayal of a trusted friend or loved ones or associate, or the life event you never expected to happen to you. It may have been the sickness that came out of nowhere and everyone forsake you in your deepest time of need. It may have been when you reached out to someone to hear your brokenness, and no one responded. It may have been the test you studied so hard for, and you still missed the mark. It may have been the loss of a loved one that you prayed so fervently would be healed. Whatever the life situation was, it obviously could not take you out and the Holy Spirit saw fit for you to be holding this very book in your hand to tell you that the best of your days is not behind you, but ahead of you. You have made it thus far and you will not quit on your destiny that God has for you. In 2 Kings 6:15-17, "Go, find out where he is," the king ordered, "so I can send men and capture him." The report came back: "He is in Dothan." Then he sent horses and chariots and a strong force there.

They went by night and surrounded the city. When the servant of the man of God got up and went out early the next morning, an army with horses and chariots had surrounded the city. "Oh, my Lord, what shall we do?" the servant asked. "Don't be afraid," the prophet answered. "Those who are with us are more than those who are with them." And Elisha prayed, "O Lord, open his eyes so he may see." Then the Lord opened the servant's eyes, and he looked and saw the hills full of horses and chariots of fire all around Elisha." Has the pain in you lasted much longer than you have anticipated? I have two words for you— fear not. You must realize that there is more to you in this fight for your life, destiny and the Chosen call of God. If you have been in much pain then you must find words to communicate that pain, hurt and disappointment. Those painful experiences are what God will use to catapult you to your next level and dimension in Him. I know that is not what you want to hear right now. You have been broken beyond recognition and you feel like you have been poured out and there is nothing left for you to give. You are completely empty, and you need God to come and breathe new life in you, right at this very moment.

It would be wise for you to hold on and take courage from this familiar passage found in Hebrews 4:15 KJV, "For we have not a high priest which cannot be touched with the feeling of our infirmities; but was in all points tempted like as we are, yet without sin." Oh, what a blessing it is at a time when nothing can bring you comfort from the pain of being so depleted but when you take hold of God's beautiful, healing and life transforming words— oh, what healing it brings to our souls! It reminds me of the song - What A

Friend We Have In Jesus, written by Joseph M. Scriven. The verse, impeccably worded, says, "What a friend we have in Jesus, all our pains and grieves to bear; what a privilege to carry everything to God in prayer; oh what peace we often forfeit; oh what needless pain we bear all because we do not carry everything to God in prayer." The words of this song do not disregard the pain and burden you have had to carry, it simply lets you know that you have a friend that is not willing to let you carry the load of these pains alone. He will not ask you for anything in exchange, He simply wants to give you the abundant life that He died on the cross for you to have. In Psalms 27:10 KJV, "When my father and my mother forsake me, then the LORD will take me up." You mean that even if the very ones who should have nurtured you missed the mark, that God Himself would take me up and wrap me in His arms and comfort me like no earthly parents, guardian, friends, brother, sister could ever do for me? Yes, He cares so much for you that He has numbered the very hair on your head. You mean more to your Heavenly Father than everything He has ever created. He calls you the apple of His eyes.

The pain you have experienced or are experiencing is to take you to a place beyond yourself, where you extend yourself to God and allow His love and healing virtue to flow through you. He will make every broken and crooked place in your life straight, fit and completely whole so that He can use your story for His story, and for His Glory. You may have tried to deal with the pain on your own, but you don't have to. God's words say that He is indeed a friend that sticketh closer than a brother or sister, or anyone and anything for that matter.

Bring all of your hurt, pain, and disappointment to your Heavenly Father. He alone will be able to understand your pain like no one else can. He has all the right remedies to soothe every area you have ever been broken. He can and will put you back together again. You have searched from place to place, from thing to thing, from person to person and nothing or no one has been able to bring you much hope, love, peace and joy.

God wants to do that for you today. He can heal you from the residue of any pain or trauma. The truth is God, not only can but it is His heart's desire towards you that you be free from every stigma of pain that has tried to keep you from bondage. It's time for you to come out screaming that you have been made free because the word of God declares in John 8:36 KJV, "If the Son therefore shall make you free, ye shall be free indeed." You mean I don't have to stay in my stage of depression, suppression or oppression? That the pain that I feel does not have to own me? That I have a right as a child of the Most High God and I can take kingdom authority, along with my praise, prayer and worship and not stay in this nasty, disgusting state? We read in God's word that God's Chosen servant David encouraged himself in the Lord. You too, have that same right and privilege as a God's Chosen child to execute your kingdom rights. Therefore, as you go forth right now with a shout of praise resounding from the crown of your head to the soles of your feet, you have given the enemy of your soul an eviction notice that your days of bondage are over.

God will require you to let go of old associations or ties that He cannot allow you to take to the next stage of your life. He has given you victory from the things that the enemy of your soul wanted to use to kill, steal and destroy you. Acknowledge the pain those separations will bring. Cry your last tear over them and take up your cross. Follow Jesus to your Chosen road and destiny. It will be worth all of the pain and trials that you have had to go through. For it is written in the word of God in 1 Corinthians 2:9 KJV, "But as it is written, Eye hath not seen, nor ear heard, neither have entered into the heart of man, the things which God hath prepared for them that love him." Therefore, God has promised to bring you joy for all of your pain. He has promised that for every painful event that you have encountered, that you can take with you from this day forth and allow God's words to minister to your aching soul, as only He can to bring the relief you have been crying out for. It starts today and you don't ever have to revisit this road again. You can now be an extension of God's arms to help bring someone else out of their deep wounds and into God's tender and healing hands. It's your time to live the life God has in store for you. Cease this God given moment with everything you have, it's your divine time to be completely free from all bondage and you do not need to look back for anyone's or anything's approval. I will say it again, it is your time! ***Let us proceed...***

CHAPTER-4
THE ISOLATION TRUTH

Webster's dictionary defines isolation as: separated from other persons or things; alone; solitary. To set or place apart, detach or separate so as to be alone. You may be saying to yourself, that does not sound too far off from where God has me right now. The moment I said an authentic 'Yes' to the Lord, it seemed like everything, and everyone was being stripped from me. I thought I had joined a solitude club. You may have asked yourself, "Why is all that I have come to know, as a source of comfort, being taken away from me?" Nothing seems to make any sense. What you thought you could not live without; God is asking you to surrender those very things. You may ask, "How can I do that? I don't want to be without a lifeline. These people have become my go-to peeps. I have been in this home now for over 20 years. I had plans to retire from my current job. I wanted to marry this individual that I have dated now for 7 years. Why is He asking me to leave all that I'm familiar with to follow Him?"

It feels unfair but we need to re-evaluate this constant demand of staying attached to things that feel as though they have no serious threat in our lives. I remember thinking that God gave me partnership in this Chosen journey when I decided to answer His call on my life. So far all I have experienced is constant heartache, brokenness and abandonment of everything I hold dear to me. I needed to have a clear understanding from the Lord. I felt as though this place of isolation, solitude and desolation was not what I signed up for. It is a lonely place to be and His word said that He promised me a land flowing with milk and honey, filled with good things full of abundance. So why does this Chosen journey feel like a place of barrenness, emptiness, loneliness, and full of dread? What is going on? The only thing I wanted to do was scream at the top of my lungs, "Help me!"

A life of isolation can fall into two categories. The first category is that you can be in a room filled with people and you still feel isolated. You are in this room where everyone is having a good time; from the outside looking in you fit the profile, based on the people that are around you. When the truth is you are sleeping in your car, have not eaten in days and you are not quite sure where your next meal is coming from. You are spending time at the feet of Jesus crying and trying to figure out, Lord did I miss you? You have separated me and isolated me from my loved ones, who although have emotionally wounded me, they simultaneously fill an emptiness in me. So, you keep on reasoning with God. The second category is that you will be stripped of everything you considered near and dear to you because of this very scripture, Luke 9:57-62 KJV. "And it came to pass, that, as they went in the way, a certain man said unto him, Lord, I will follow thee whithersoever thou goest. And Jesus said unto him, Foxes have holes, and birds of the air have nests; but the Son of man hath not where to lay his head. And he said unto another, Follow me.

But he said, Lord, suffer me first to go and bury my father. Jesus said unto him, Let the dead bury their dead: but go thou and preach the kingdom of God. And another also said, Lord, I will follow thee; but let me first go bid them farewell, which are at home at my house. And Jesus said unto him, no man, having put his hand to the plough, and looking back, is fit for the kingdom of God." As you can see, even the Son of Man had no place to lay His head. Jesus had to leave everything He knew. The comfort of His mother and family. The call and cost to follow Christ, if you are authentic about fulfilling the call of God on your life, it will cost you everything. Now your salvation is a free gift given to you from the Lord, for the great and tremendous price He paid for our lives on the cross. The cost to walk in the kingdom's principles and destiny of God as stated in Matthew 6:33 KJV, "But seek first his kingdom and his righteousness, and all these things will be given to you as well."

God desires to bless your full obedience. This scripture is not just a nice phrase, it is the divine will and purpose of your Heavenly Father for your life. The call is not for those who long to walk in the path that is straight and wide, but it is a call to walk uncompromisingly the narrow path that is destined for all of God's Chosen vessels. Those who have an ear to hear when the Spirit of the Lord is calling them, just like the Apostle John and all of God's fervent servants in the bible. Come Higher as found in Revelation 4:1-4 KJV, "After this I looked, and, behold, a door was opened in heaven: and the first voice which I heard was as it were of a trumpet talking with me; which said, Come up hither, and I will shew thee things which must be hereafter. And immediately I was in the spirit: and behold, a throne was set in heaven, and one sat on the throne. And he that sat was to look upon like a jasper and a sardine stone: and there was a rainbow round about the throne, in sight like unto an emerald. And round about the throne were four and twenty seats: and upon the seats I saw four and twenty elders sitting, clothed in white raiment; and they had on their head's crowns of gold."

God has indeed placed you in total isolation from loved ones, ties of friendship and associates. Even the very person you use to talk to everyday about the things of the Lord, is no longer available when you call. God has asked you to relocate to a city, a church, a new job and a new environment where you don't know anyone. However, trying it has been for you, it is because the Father will use this isolation process to take you to a place of higher heights and deeper depths with Him. As God's Chosen one you must willingly and wholeheartedly obey the voice of your Heavenly Father because you have a relationship with Him and not just head knowledge of Him. You must decide to comply with God's voice, after all, in John 10:27 KJV, "My sheep hear My voice, and I know them, and they follow Me." Therefore, you follow the voice of your Heavenly Father with a confidence that makes you go through your season of isolation, with great trust and faith; that if God has called you to this the Holy Spirit will continue to assure you that you are going to make it and that this process too shall pass. You will come out refined, renewed and ready to be all that God wants you to be. You must know that this process of isolation from your Heavenly Father was never meant to harm you and take you away from the comforts that you have become accustomed to. No, it is to allow you to go into a place of intimacy with Him where all other voices of distraction may be blocked out.

In the natural world, when we are isolated from others, it is never a loving and welcoming process because God created us to have fellowship with one another. However, for the truest form of fellowship and relationship to be effective, it must first start with your Heavenly Father. He desires to commune with you. If you are too busy tending to everything else, His voice becomes like a faint whisper resounding from a distance. Isolation in the eyes of God makes no sense to the natural mind. It resembles a husband and wife coming together in intimacy, as only they can effectively minister to one another in the purest form of love. It is the same when God calls His Chosen one apart because He is a God of intimacy and He longs very much to fellowship with you, as He did with Adam in the cool of the day found in Genesis 3:8 KJV. "And they heard the sound of the LORD God walking in the garden in the cool of the day, and Adam and his wife hid themselves from the presence of the LORD God among the trees of the garden."

God does not want us to hide from Him. He is calling out to you today and saying, where are you? He desires to fellowship with us but in all of our busyness, along with the other idols that we put in front of Him, we hardly notice how God has now become a secondary place in our lives and hearts. But in God's unfailing love and grace, we find that God so longs fellowship with you, so much that He will interrupt your plans if He has to. Your cell phone will stop working, your close and dear friends begin to disappear, the job that you depended on so much will begin to change. God wants your attention, and He will obtain it. Whether it is through you obeying His voice simply or having to be stripped of everything that is a distraction between you and Him. We find that in Corinthians 11:2 KJV, "For I am jealous for you with a godly jealousy; for I betrothed you to one husband, so that to Christ I might present you as a pure virgin." What a wonderful feeling to know that God is jealous for you so much that He will not stop pursuing your affection, even if it means He has to isolate you from the things or people that are keeping you away from His plan, purpose and divine destiny for your life.

This authentic and amazing love from God can only be experienced in its fullness when you allow God, Himself, to take you through His isolation process where no one will ever be able to come between you and the intimacy that you and your Heavenly Father have obtained. It will cost you everything. You will cry, you will be lonely, and you will wonder if you are being punished for something you did. The nights will feel very long and weary but know that at the end that the price that you paid will not and can never be taken from you by anyone or anything ever again. Go forth on your Chosen Journey, not of isolation with your Lord, but of pure love and intimacy like you have never known before. *Let us proceed...*

CHAPTER-5
THE FORGOTTEN TRUTH

Is this where you are God's Chosen one? Have you been living life day by day and trying to keep up with the best of them? Everyone around you is moving forward and you're trying to simply maintain while knowing good and well that each step you take, unknown to the rest of them, takes everything within you. You just want to fall by the waste side and make the declaration that your journey ends here. Enough is enough! I know there are times in your Chosen journey that you have asked yourself, "why am I doing this again? No one seems to care, hear me or see me. Day and night, I am going through the routine smiling at everyone when on the inside I am a mess, broken, wounded beyond measure." Or so the enemy of your soul wants you to believe. Well, the life of God's Chosen one was never said to be easy or simple, but the good news is that there is hope. You don't have to stay in your condition and God will make a way of escape if you shall seek him with all of your heart, mind, body, spirit and soul. Webster defines forgotten as: to be unable to remember something; to treat with thoughtless intention; I neglect: to leave behind unintentionally; to fail to mention; to banish from one's thoughts. Have these been your past or current experiences with God? Have you felt forgotten by those who should have loved and celebrated you? Maybe friends who promised to be there, turned their back on you. Maybe your children, spouse, boss, coworker, church family have decided that you are not worth a second thought and what you have to say is of no importance.

Not only is your heart breaking toward those different life scenarios, now you look at God who says in His word in Numbers 23:19 KJV, "God is not a man, that he should lie; neither the son of man, that he should repent: hath he said, and shall he not do it? Or hath he spoken, and shall he not make it good?" Well, Lord, here it is! In your own words, that you are not a man that you should lie. Well, everything I have been going through has appeared to be a contradiction to your word God?. I love you but I am not seeing the promises in my life come to pass, Lord. I have been in this cycle or season of just sowing and believing. Yes, at times, wavering because I don't know what to do. Is there really help for me? Is this just a tradition that I have been following? Why do I feel so forgotten? It has been 2 years,

10 years and now 20 years, when is this sick cycle going to end?

Those are valuable questions and God wants to meet you right where you are to answer every one of your questions. Please rest assure, He is not an unfair or unjust God that will leave you in a state of limbo or confusion because the Bible clearly states in 1 Corinthians 14:33 KJV, "For God is not the author of confusion, but of peace, as in all churches of the saints." While what you are feeling and experiencing may not have originated from God Himself, He can use the situation that the enemy of your soul sent to keep you in defeat. You need to know that God will turn it around and use it for His glory. To be forgotten or overlooked is not a feeling any one of us, whether as one Chosen vessel or one who has not yet made Jesus Christ their personal Lord and Savior, ever wants to experience. It's a lonely and devastating place to be when you feel like you are in a crowd of people, but no one seems to notice or care about you. You can understand if you did something to offend them or you were not available when they needed you, but like God's Servant David states in Psalm 55 12-14 KJV, "If an enemy was insulting me, I could endure it; if a foe were raising himself against me, I could hide from him. But it is you, a man like myself, my companion, my close friend, with whom I once enjoyed sweet fellowship as we walked with the throng at the house of God."

You considered them your closest friends who should have been there when you lost your loved one, when your house went into foreclosure, when everyone lied to you, or when your marriage fell apart. They promised to be there with you but now that everything in your life is falling apart, they are nowhere to be found. You are left to fend for yourself and are forgotten by those whom you thought would always be there. But there is comfort for you today, found in the word of the Lord in Psalm 118: 8-9 KJV, "It is better to trust in the Lord than to put confidence in man. It is better to trust in the Lord than to put confidence in princes; (men)." What a revelation to know that men in all their good intentions will forget you, they will fail you, but God in His infinite grace, mercy and abundance of love will never lead us astray. However, if we are willing to take Him at his word, He will bring us back to the right path no matter how much you have had to go through.

He is faithful and will fulfill all of His good thoughts and intentions towards you as stated in Jeremiah 29:11 KJV, "For I know the thoughts that I think toward you, saith the LORD, thoughts of peace, and not of evil, to give you an expected end."

Let's look closer at one of God's Chosen daughters in the Bible, who knew what it was like to be forgotten. In Mark 5: 25-34 KJV, "And a certain woman, which had an issue of blood twelve years, and had suffered many things of many physicians, and had spent all that she had, and was nothing bettered, but rather grew worse, When she had heard of Jesus, came in the press behind, and touched his garment. For she said, If I may touch his clothes, I shall be whole. And straightway the fountain of her blood was dried up; and she felt in her body that she was healed of that plague. And Jesus, immediately knowing in himself that virtue had gone out of him, turned him about in the press, and said, who touched my clothes? And his disciples said unto him, Thou seest the multitude thronging thee, and sayest thou, Who touched me? And he looked round about to see her that had done this thing. But the woman, fearing and trembling, knowing what was done in her, came and fell down before him, and told him all the truth. And he said unto her, Daughter, thy faith hath made thee whole; go in peace and be whole of thy plague." Now let me ask you, God's Chosen one, can you relate to this precious daughter who carried the pain of feeling forgotten for twelve long excruciating years? The fact that you are reading this book is a divine sign that God in His merciful and loving heart has not forgotten you. He wants you to know, the same way a special day was set aside for His Chosen daughter, He has the same healing and deliverance reserve for you and all of His sons and daughters who may feel that they have been forgotten or forsaken. Truth be told, there are a lot of lessons that we can learn from this mighty and powerful Chosen vessel of God. Let us look further into her story. The word of the Lord states in Mark 5: 25-34, "And a certain woman, which had an issue of blood twelve years, And had suffered many things of many physicians, and had spent all that she had, and was nothing bettered, but rather grew worse, When she had heard of Jesus, came in the press behind, and touched his garment. For she said, if I may touch but his clothes, I shall be whole and straight away the fountain of her blood was dried up; and she felt in her body that she was healed of that plague." She had an issue with her blood for over twelve years. She sought many physicians and spent all that she had, but it only grew worse.

What has been the issue of blood in your life? Does your leak in life resemble a Chosen journey, where everything and everyone in life seems to just be taking from you with no reciprocation? In the medical world, blood represents life. That's why when you donate blood, you are helping to give life to someone else. But what happens when the very blood that should bring you life, keeps leaking out of you? To some, that may represent the marriage that you are in everyday. Striving to be a good wife or a good husband, however, nothing seems good enough. You try to be the perfect child so that you will be accepted in the family, but nothing seems to be working, your parents still want more from you. Things only grow worse. Everyone wants more from you, but they don't even have the capacity to remember your full name most days.

When will I stop leaking? When will someone really help me and not take advantage of me? When will Jesus truly come to my rescue? Like the woman with the issue of blood, you have run out of every resource. You have run out of people showing you sympathy now because you have nothing more to give. They completely forget about you, and you have become a nuisance and a distance memory. Oh, how sad God's Chosen daughter must have felt. What did she have to live for? However, if you think this is the end for you and this precious Chosen daughter of God, you could not be more wrong. The word continues by saying that, "when she heard Jesus she said to herself, Heavenly Father give all of your Chosen ones an ear to hear when you are passing by, and the ability to open their mouth and decree a thing and see it establish according to your word and will for their lives. She went, as she pressed her way through the crowd, in all of her weakness and frailty, this daughter mustered up all the faith and strength she had. She was determined to not miss her divine appointment with the only one who could do anything about her long and drawn-out condition. This Chosen Daughter knew she was tired of being taken advantage by others and most of all, she was tired of being forgotten. She knew there was more to life than her being a leaking faucet, where all of her life supplies and energy, day in and day out, was being taken from her.

Some days, she did all she could to get out of bed. Her tears were also in constant leaking mode. Her heart was faint and breaking inside of her all at the same time. She certainly would have pondered the question: what did I do to deserve such treatment, when will it come to a stop? Well, she faithfully decided she was going to press her way through and if she could only touch the hem of Jesus' garment, even if she gets stomped on or pushed down, she had made up her mind to move forward and nothing was going to stop her now. Let us see what occurred next to this Chosen vessel, in Mark 5: 25-34 KJV, "For she said, If I may touch but his clothes, I shall be whole. And straightway the fountain of her blood was dried up; and she felt in her body that she was healed of that plague. And Jesus, immediately knowing in himself that virtue had gone out of him, turned him about in the press, and said, who touched my clothes? And his disciples said unto him, Thou seest the multitude thronging thee, and sayest thou, Who touched me? And he looked round about to see her that had done this thing.

But the woman, fearing and trembling, knowing what was done to her, came and fell down before him, and told him all the truth. And he said unto her, Daughter, thy faith hath made thee whole; go in peace, and be whole of thy plague."

There are miracles of healing and comfort being released to you, as you are reading this book. It is a prophetic confirmation and proclamation that God is touching you just like this beautiful daughter, 'Jesus has not nor could He ever forget about you. She pressed on and touched Jesus. Jesus turned around and asked who touched Him, because He felt power leave His body and He did not authorize that power. The Chosen daughter, knowing that her healing had been manifested, was no longer a forgotten outcast by her family or society because of the sickness she carried for so long. With shaking and trembling legs, she knew that if Jesus was asking who touched Him, she had better come clean so she could be in order and publicly give her testimony to seal her healing. She was no longer going to be denied, ignored, labeled, forgotten nor forsaken, this was her day of coming back to her rightful position. She was not going to let the fear, or the opinions of what others had to say, deny her of her God divine Chosen moment.

In the meantime, the disciples who were with Jesus, thought He was going crazy in a crowd filled with people where everyone is touching one another, to ask who touched him. The word goes on to tell us she knew what had happened to her, immediately, not days, weeks nor months or even years later, but she was instantly healed. So, she had to confess to Jesus and the entire crowd what had just transpired in her and through her, after suffering for twelve long years. Jesus then looked at her with such love and compassion and said to her "thy faith has made thee whole, go in peace and be whole of thy plague." What is the plague that has you so bound that you feel that these very words which Jesus spoke to His Chosen daughter cannot be applied to your situation for however long your Chosen journey has been? God is not mocked, and He is not in the business of showing favoritism. The fact that you are reading this book is a sure sign He wants you to be free from everything that would come to tell you that you will remain in your stage of bondage forever. The devil is a liar and the father of all lies. You have the power, as did this beautiful chosen daughter, to press with every ounce of faith that you can muster up, open your mouth and make the declaration that you will not stay in the condition that has come to overshadow you.

The word shadow is defined here as: an area that is not or is only partially irradiated or illuminated because of the interception of radiation by an opaque object between the area and the source of radiation; a feeling or cause of gloom or unhappiness: an imperfect imitation or copy. The enemy wants to keep you in complete darkness by trying to block the light of illumination between you and your Heavenly Father. You have the power with your faith and the word of God to speak to the shadow of the enemy that is lurking around you and trying to keep you from seeing the truth, that you have not been forgotten and you carry the greater anointing to destroy the work of the enemy in every circumstance and situation in your life. You may have felt forgotten however, God's Chosen one, it is now time to turn the table at the enemy of your soul and at your adversary and boldly declare to him, with a voice of triumph "FORGET YOU." I choose this day that I will not be the forgotten one because my Heavenly Father has decided that He will never leave me or forsake me. At this very moment, I place the blood of Jesus to overshadow me and to stop all of the enemies' darkness from following me and having any access to me in all areas of my life. You will no longer be able to block or keep the light of Jesus from penetrating my entire soul, mind, spirit and body that I may illuminate ever so brightly in the presence of everyone and everywhere that I go.

I declare that I am a carrier of God's glorious light, and nothing will take that from me anymore. Satan, you are now on notice I am taking Jesus at His word, but I am going to shine with all the brightness that my Heavenly Father has imparted in me. I take this moment to send God's light to shine ever so brightly your way. This divine blindness is God's reward to you and everyone connected to you, and for the "fire" of God to come down and consume you completely. I proclaim to you this day, that the same tenacity and courage and strength that overcame this Chosen daughter, as we have recently read in the word of God, has now come upon you too. Just like her, you too have the ability to hear Jesus calling you out of your forgotten state, press through all of the lies that you have come into agreement with from the enemy of your soul. You now have your God's given authority to confidently, boldly and courageously touch Jesus with your Faith by speaking His word to your situation. Then you will hear your Heavenly Father say to you just like in Mark 5: 25-34 KJV, "Daughter, thy faith hath made thee whole; go in peace and be whole of thy plague." God has set up this divine moment just for you, for you are His Chosen vessel; it is vital that you know that it's God's honor to meet you right where we are. *Let us proceed*...

CHAPTER-6
THE SURRENDERING TRUTH

What is it that your Heavenly Father is asking you to surrender today? If you want to live a full life, then you must be sure to know that there is a process of surrendering that will take place. The price of a surrendered vessel will cost you everything that is dear to you, at least in your infinite mind. But God in His surpassing wisdom will not let you live beneath the life He has orchestrated for you, and He will be sure that you will also gain everything in Him that He has destined for you. It's only a loss when you are not willing to be obedient and surrender that which your Heavenly Father is requiring and asking of you. For it is God who gave it all to you in the first place. Let's look at this particular passage in Genesis 22: 3-12 KJV, "Sometime later God tested Abraham. He said to him, "Abraham!" "Here I am," he replied. Then God said, "Take your son, your only son, Isaac, whom you love, and go to the region of Moriah. Sacrifice him there as a burnt offering on one of the mountains I will tell you about." Early the next morning Abraham got up and saddled his donkey. He took with him two of his servants and his son Isaac. When he had cut enough wood for the burnt offering, he set out for the place God had told him about. On the third day Abraham looked up and saw the place in the distance. He said to his servants, "Stay here with the donkey while I and the boy go over there. We will worship and then we will come back to you." Abraham took the wood for the burnt offering and placed it on his son Isaac, and he himself carried the fire and the knife. As the two of them went on together, Isaac spoke up and said to his father Abraham, "Father?" "Yes, my son?" Abraham replied. "The fire and wood are here," Isaac said, "but where is the lamb for the burnt offering?" Abraham answered, "God himself will provide the lamb for the burnt offering, my son." And the two of them went on together. When they reached the place God had told him about, Abraham built an altar there and arranged the wood on it. He bound his son Isaac and laid him on the altar, on top of the wood. Then he reached out his hand and took the knife to slay his son. But the angel of the LORD called out to him from heaven, "Abraham! Abraham!" "Here I am," he replied. "Do not lay a hand on the boy," he said. "Do not do anything to him. Now I know that you fear God, because you have not withheld from me your son, your only son."

Wow, you mean that after God granted His servant Abraham the promise of His son Isaac, he then turned around and told him to sacrifice his son to Him? How many of you would conclude that Abraham must have 80 asked himself if He was truly hearing God. How could that happen? Why would God ask for that? The Bible does not mention any arguments from Abraham however, we can place ourselves in Abraham's shoes for a moment and imagine the various emotions you would be experiencing at this point especially being a Chosen vessel who is sold out for the Lord? You would, of course, say 'yes' just like Abraham did, however on the other side of your untold story would certainly include how your tears flowed nonstop, all the while your heart is breaking in half. Yet, the strange and comforting thing is in your state blind faith you still have this peace and strength to walk that mountain and do all what your God has asked of you. This is the peace of God the bible speaks of, that passes all understanding. God's peace is nothing like the temporary peace of this world. Therefore, this means that the same thing that you are going through may be happening to someone else, but God's grace and mercy will take you through it and make sure you see the light at the end of the tunnel.

I know that God's promise to you has been delayed, and it may feel so far back that you think that vision has taken root on some stony ground and will never be resurrected again. It feels like no one else around you had to surrender anything at all, except for you. Your name seems to be the name always being picked during the sacrifice and surrendering drawings. You try to bargain things out with God, pleading for Him to pick Sister Mary or Brother Job this time instead. Well, God is God all by Himself and He can pick whomever He wants and ask them to surrender whatever He wants, the only question is will you be obedient quickly in your surrendering process so that God can bring your best into existence.

You may have been living comfortably in a good situation, but God wants to take you from a better life to the best life. Stop fighting the urge to simply live in contentment, God wants to take you higher and deeper in Him. It was not an easy decision for God's Servant Abraham to make given the cost, but he made it in order to receive God's blessing. Consider this, if Abraham did not surrender and obey the Lord, he would have remained in the state of complacency while God was trying to simply multiply his chosen blessings upon his life. Our God is truly a promise keeper of multiplication and increase. We can see this in Genesis 1:22 KJV, "And God blessed them, saying, "Be fruitful and multiply, and fill the waters in the seas, and let birds multiply on the earth." You see when the Lord asks you to surrender, He wants to add something to you and not to take something away from you, which is why He is a God of multiplication and addition and not a God of division and subtraction.

I know there is something in your life that looks good and they may not even be sins, However God is asking you to give him that very thing. If it is a thought that you cannot fathom why God is asking this of you, then those things may just be a crutch for you to lean on. They may not actually be for you. Whether it is your significant partner who tells you how special you are, or your child that you have been holding on to. When God is saying like Hannah, in the book of Samuel, I will grant you your request but can I trust you to offer it back to me wholeheartedly? That house, car, job, ministry, business, the college you want to get into so badly, would you give that very thing right back to God? The longer you hold on, the louder God will speak to you so that you do not miss His blessings that will bring greater increase into your life. You see in John 12:24 KJV, " Verily, verily, I say unto you, except a corn of wheat falls into the ground and dies, it abideth alone: but if it dies, it bringeth forth much fruit. Sometimes the very thing that you believe God brought to you is the very thing.

He will require back from you. As you continue on your Chosen journey you will come to understand to never hold anything so closely that you can't give it back to your Heavenly Father when He asks for that very thing back because all things belong to Him. You are only a steward of these things. He only entrusts you with.

Let's revisit Abraham and see what happens next as he completely surrenders to the will of God. In Genesis 22: 13-18 KJV, "And Abraham lifted up his eyes, and looked, and behold behind him a ram caught in a thicket by his horns: and Abraham went and took the ram and offered him up for a burnt offering in the stead of his son. And Abraham called the name of that place Jehovah Jireh: as it is said to this day, In the mount of the Lord it shall be seen. And the angel of the Lord called unto Abraham out of heaven the second time, And said, By myself have I sworn, saith the Lord, for because thou hast done this thing, and hast not withheld thy son, thine only son: That in blessing I will bless thee, and in multiplying I will multiply thy seed as the stars of the heaven, and as the sand which is upon the seashore; and thy seed shall possess the gate of his enemies; And in thy seed shall all the nations of the earth be blessed; because thou hast obeyed my voice." God's Chosen one, when you surrender all that God is asking that you hold dear to, it is then you will find that your Heavenly Father truly does not withhold any good and perfect thing from you.

When God asks you to give up that which is of much value to you, it is best to believe He is testing to see if you will surrender or hold on to the very thing that He wants to use to bring increase and multiplication into your life. I know you may be trying to justify why you can't give those things up, but God is telling you with a gentle or loud whisper that He has not selected any of these things for you. So then what do you do? You learn to become a master at the art of letting go and letting God have His good and perfect way in you and through you. God wants to perfect your faith along with your complete trust in Him. He was never trying to harm you or take anything away from you. All He needs is for you to put a mustard seed of faith and action with your full divine understanding of who He is in your life, and with your willingness and obedience to surrender to that which He is calling you to completely and wholeheartedly. So, you can now stop crying about why your neighbor two blocks down the street keeps getting blessed and you are still in the same predicament you were in 2 years ago. Something is happening and it does not make sense to the natural mind, but it is aligning itself in the spiritual realms instead and the natural realm will follow God's sovereign guidance. You see some things that are in the spiritual world are not always going to make sense to the natural mind, however, when both the natural realm and the spiritual realm are in opposition this would indicate that you are operating out of the will and purpose of God.

Take a look at what happens when you stop fighting God and walk in God's total surrender in Genesis 22: 13-18 KJV, "And Abraham lifted up his eyes, and looked, and behold behind him a ram caught in a thicket by his horns: and Abraham went and took the ram, and offered him up for a burnt offering in the stead of his son. And Abraham called the name of that place Jehovah Jireh: as it is said to this day, in the mount of the Lord it shall be seen". Abraham was offered a ram by God instead of having to sacrifice his son. God made a covenant with him to multiply his seeds as the stars and the sand off the seashore. Now that's a lot of stars and sand! God promised him that his seed shall possess the gate of his enemies. These are not little promises, this is the greater increase and multiplication that you have been waiting for, which God Himself has promised to you. We know that God's ways are not our ways, so if He is asking you to surrender something that is important to you and dear to you, then that means that it is as important to God to have your complete surrender and obedience to His voice and instructions. The very moment that you do fully surrender, He will give you back what you thought you had lost and make it a manifold blessing in your life that will multiply many times over.

The hurt of surrendering and letting go, of that which the Lord is asking of you, will not be a pain of devastation because, Chosen one, He will fill the void and make it bearable until He brings to pass that which He truly wants to bless you with. Because God truly does make everything beautiful in His perfect and marvelous timing. *Let us proceed...*

CHAPTER-7
THE BITTERNESS TRUTH

Webster's Dictionary defines bitterness as: characterized by strong feelings of hatred, resentment, cynicism; causing or showing sorrow, discomfort, or pain; grievous etc. This does not sound like the definition or characteristics that God's Chosen ones should be carrying around. Whether or not you are in God's Chosen elect, or just thinking about coming to the Kingdom of your Heavenly Father, no one is exempt from going through the difficulties of life experiences and struggles. Let's look at what God's word has to say about bitterness and His warning to us who are His Chosen sons and daughters when faced with such emotions in Hebrews 12:15 NIV, "See to it that no one fails to obtain the grace of God; that no "root of bitterness" springs up and causes trouble, and by it many become defiled." Let's look in Deuteronomy 29:18 NIV, "Make sure there is no man or woman, clan or tribe among you today whose heart turns away from the Lord our God to go and worship the gods of those nations; make sure there is no root among you that produces such bitter poison.

The Lord will never be willing to forgive him; his wrath and zeal will burn against that man. All the curses written in this book will fall upon him and the Lord will blot out his name from under heaven." Wow, you mean to say this issue of bitterness is that important to our Heavenly Father? You might be saying right now, I had no idea it would cause such a devastating effect. You would think the best thing to do is to not be in the proximity of a person who has hurt you would be enough. The hurt they caused may feel unforgivable however, the scripture above strongly warns us not to harbor bitterness in our hearts, with our fellowmen, our family members, or holding grudges against those in God's house or worse you just forget about God altogether because you choose to harbor the spirit of bitterness within you. You may be saying right now, "but you don't know how much this person has caused me harm! Why should I allow them such access to me, so they can cause me more pain?" Letting go of any bitterness that you are carrying towards yourself based on something you may have done to someone else, or you are carrying a heart of bitterness because someone you love has hurt you deeply could be the hardest process to let go and move on from.

How bad do you want to be free from the pain of your past, or the pain of your present situation? Only you can give a genuine answer to those questions and see God's grace, in the above scripture in Hebrews 12:15, states that bitterness as it begins to manifest itself into its fullness, in order for it not to take root and become a deadly poison that spreads throughout your entire body and causes you to die an early death. Let me ask you, can you look back and trace the date and place where your bitterness originated from? Was it from an abusive physical and verbal relationship? Was it from the hand of someone you trusted, and they betrayed you beyond comprehension? Was it a parent or guardian who never built you up but just constantly put you down with negative words? All of us have been hurt, abused, neglected, abandoned, forsaken, and mishandled. You see at one point in our lives each of us lived through those negative feelings. Those scars do not heal overnight and sometimes not at all, unless you allow God complete personal access to come and deal with the broken and depleted places in your life.

Bitterness, if not dealt with, will take its toll on you. You'll become numb and everything will feel the same or maybe you won't feel anything at all. You simply only exist but are not living the full life that God has designed for you. Your ability to enjoy the everyday things in life such as laughter, love, a walk in the park, the company of those whom you used to be able to fellowship with has become dull. Life has become mundane and filled with dreadful days which only brings sadness and pain beyond what your words can articulate. You start to feel like everything, and everyone seems to be acting negatively towards you, and every word seems to be an attack on you as well as on your very character. When you start looking at things through the eyes of a bitter person, no one can do anything right in your eyes. You become the master controller of your environment and you begin to operate in the spirit of pride. Pride comes with a mind state of 'this is my territory, if you don't like how I run it, feel free to leave. I don't have time for people who can't see things my way. I don't need you here.' As believable as those following statements may sound, let's just be honest, what you are really crying out for is someone to see all of the pain and manipulation which you have so quietly endured, for them to come in and take your hand from this place of bitterness. Someone with the boldness and tenacity to break to all of the rough interior and the act of stubbornness that you are exacerbating.

You are, indeed, shouting for someone to please dare to come in and help you get all this filthiness out of you. Let's go on and examine the scripture below. In the Book of Ephesians 4:29-32 KJV, "Let no corrupt word proceed out of your mouth, but what is good for necessary edification, that it may impart grace to the hearers. And do not grieve the Holy Spirit of God, by whom you were sealed for the day of redemption. Let all bitterness, wrath, anger, clamor, and evil speaking be put away from you, with all malice. And be kind to one another, tenderhearted, forgiving one another, even as God in Christ forgave you." Walking in deep bitterness allows all the filth to come into your spirit and that brings no good thing to you except a cold heart that grieves the Holy Spirit. The bible clearly says that we are to walk in forgiveness and love towards one another and be at peace with your fellow men as much as you possibly can. A popular scripture, in the word of God, teaches us that "shaking the dust from your feet" can best be explained as to shake the animosity and bitter feelings which arose between others and yourself, as you leave their very presence. So that you may go on your way, with your heart full of peace and joy, as God's Chosen should.

You must never take with you the dust of hatred and resentment; shake it off and leave it behind so you may continue to walk with a pure heart. The bitterness that you carry in your heart is not being taken lightly at all in this book. You may have had a situation happen to you that was so bitter that you feel like if you forgive, let go and release it, your perpetrator has gotten away with hurting and mistreating you.

In your infinite mind, you decide the best way for you to get revenge is to make them pay by keeping the act constantly in the forefront of your mind because it would be a hot day in the North pole before this situation ever happens to you again. Yet here you are telling everybody you are healed. All the while your mind is renting free space to an individual that has hurt you. Staying in this bitter condition will not give you rest; it will continue to cause the same nightmare that seems so real to constantly keep revisiting this unfortunate and bitter event for the rest of your life. God's Chosen vessel, no one or anything deserves to have that kind of access to you. It is the enemy of your soul who wants to desperately keep you in a stagnant state from receiving your complete deliverance in the area of bitterness, because he wants your heart to grow numb and cold. You have now become an unwilling participant and partner to your perpetrator.

Just how unfair does that sound? That is the plan of your adversary, to keep you bound and stay in total bondage to him so that you may never be free to live a life free of bitterness. He does not want you to enjoy anything that brings you God's best or have anything to do with the things that will bring you closer to your Heavenly Father. This root of bitterness that is rooted so deep in you does not have to become a lifestyle for you. Jesus came to set the captive free. Have you experienced a broken heart that you think is beyond repair? Have you lost someone dear to you, while you were standing in the word of God believing for their healing to come forth and they die anyway? What, or who, was it that hurt you so badly that you don't think there is enough light at the end of the tunnel for you to see your way out? I ask you again. Who did it? When did it happen? Why did it happen? These are the questions that you have been rehearsing in your head over and over again and you still come out blaming yourself and thinking that you deserve exactly all that you are now going through, oh dear chosen one, the devil is truly a liar to have your mind believing his lies and false accusations.

Let me help bring some comfort and healing to the brokenness of your heart and help you to be free of this deep bitterness. I know I am not the individual that hurt you so very deeply, however I would like to extend a deep apology on behalf of those that have directed and indirected all of their own weakness and pain on to you. Today, if you are reading this book, it's not by coincidence but the Holy Spirit knew that the words and deliverance that penetrates the pages of this book was the healing that you needed. It is your time and yes, it is certainly your season, of being free from the bondage of the bitterness of yesterday's pain. It is your time to walk into the freedom that God has for you, bountiful blessings flowing with abundant life and living waters. There is a mighty spring flowing on the inside of you as you are reading this book, it is the well of God's cleansing living water, He wants to flow to you and through you, so you can be a carrier of His authentic love, joy, and peace. Oh yes, did I mention Joy? Unspeakable Joy! I see the tears of joy that are now swelling up in your eyes, where there once used to be tears of pain and devastation. Those beautiful tears of joy are coming up from the river of living water that God is now allowing to flow through you with His sweet presence. He wants to make you a carrier of His glory, so He will never let you live in a place that is less than His very best for you. I now entrust you in the arms of the Lover of your soul, to continue to minister to you even now and finish the good work that He started in you.

God's reminder to us in the Book of Hebrews 3:12-15 KJV, " Beware, brethren, lest there be in any of you an evil heart of unbelief in departing from the living God; but exhort one another daily, while it is called "Today," lest any of you be hardened through the deceitfulness of sin. For we have become partakers of Christ if we hold the beginning of our confidence steadfast to the end, while it is said: "Today, if you will hear His voice, do not harden your hearts as in one living in rebellion." *Let us proceed...*

CHAPTER-8
THE FORGIVENESS TRUTH

Webster's Dictionary defines forgiveness as: the process of concluding resentment, indignation or anger as a result of a perceived offense, difference or mistake, and/or ceasing to demand punishment or restitution. Now let's look at what God has to say on this subject matter. The Bible clearly states in Luke 6:29 KJV, "Whoever hits you on the cheek, offer him the other also; and whoever takes away your coat, do not withhold your shirt from him either." God's definition, compared to Webster's dictionary, would appear to be a strong contradiction. However, if we look closer and follow God's way and examples on how to walk in forgiveness, one would avoid the outcomes mentioned in Webster's definition. I know some of you, like myself, currently have your mouth wide open saying, Wow! Are you for real God? You have got to be kidding! This person just slapped me in the face, spit on me, talked and lied behind my back, my marriage is falling apart, physically abused my child, and also did all kinds of evil and injustice against me.

God weren't you paying attention to any of these painful life circumstances I have just been through? God do you need to have it replayed all over for you? How can you tell me after they did all that to me, I am not only to turn my cheek, but you want me to even give them the very clothes of my back too? What am I a fool? No way! God, come on now there has got to be another way.

If we as God's Chosen ones are going to be authentic and real, that is how most of our responses would be when it comes to the question of forgiving those who have done us wrong. Forgiveness is never an easy thing for most people, we want the wrong that has been done to us to be justified. How dare they get away completely free, when I am left here with all this pain that they have caused me. You must know that in your Chosen journey, the only manual that you will have to help you march day by day toward this walk of forgiveness, is the word of God. Do well to remember that day you said, "God I choose to follow you; give me all of you and take away anything that resembles me in the equation." Your own proclamation to God that very day will come with a test that you alone will be asked to live out these very words that you have just uttered to your Heavenly Father. In Romans 5:3-5 KJV, "And not only so, but we glory in tribulations also: knowing that tribulation worketh patience; And patience, experience; and experience, hope: And hope maketh not ashamed; because the love of God is shed abroad in our hearts by the Holy Ghost which is given unto us."

We see that God is not trying to hurt or harm His Chosen ones when He asks us to walk the walk. Our elder brother Jesus, himself, had to walk His walk out in full obedience, and so we are no different as God's chosen ones. We are not greater than Jesus; He had to learn to forgive just as God asks of us to walk in forgiveness. The word of God says that in Hebrews 5: 8-9 KJV, "Though he was a Son, yet learned obedience by the things which he suffered; And being made perfect, he became the author of eternal salvation unto all of them that obey him." Yes, even Jesus had to suffer some things that He would have preferred not to have gone through. He was lied on, spit on, disfigured beyond recognition on an old rugged cross. He was despised and hated by those who should have received Him. They hated Jesus without cause. Yet, He only wanted to do the will and the purpose of His Heavenly Father. How could the Son of God who was sinless, take upon our sins that we may have eternal salvation? We must ask ourselves, what is it that we have suffered from the hands of our accusers that we are unwilling to forgive? I have heard it said that I forgive the offender, but I will never forget what they have done to me.

Many people seem to think this statement brings them out of the captivity of an unforgiving heart. Clearly, we see that God's answer to that is found in Psalms 103:12 KJV, "As far as the east is from the west, so far has He removed our transgressions from us." These words help us to get an insight and understand on how to walk in total forgiveness, you cannot hold the person's offense against them. You have to release them wholeheartedly. As Chosen vessels, we are called to walk a walk of forgiveness that is different from that of the world standards. You see the world says, 'you hurt me deeply I will cut you off and you will never hurt me again.' Unfortunately, this attitude has been seen operating not only in the world but also among some of our churches. It is a sad statement to believe that this unforgiveness trap is also happening in God's church, but it is true. That is one reason I believe the world cannot seem to make a clear distinction between the church and itself. Therefore, we misrepresent Jesus by failing to walk in the purest form of forgiveness.

There are some hurts that we experience and go through that knocks the very breath out of us. It causes us to wonder how I can ever forgive this person for raping me, aborting the child I have longed for, the church leaders for not living the life they have preached to us from the word of God, or having the one you love and trusted most walk away and leave you. How can God ask me to take these life events so lightly? Please understand Chosen vessels, as my wise and Godly Pastor always quotes, "If it is not God sent; it will certainly be God used." As hard as those above offenses are, what a liberating feeling to know that God is still in control and He has promised to take all vengeance for us, so we do not need to take it upon ourselves. We find that in Romans 12:19 KJV, "Dearly beloved, avenge not yourselves, but rather give place unto wrath: for it is written, Vengeance is mine; I will repay, saith the Lord." The Bible also tells us that what the enemy meant for evil, your God is more than able to turn it around for your good. When you refuse to forgive completely, you are cheating yourself out of God's blessings and not your perpetrator who mocks you and thinks he or she has gotten away with offending and hurting you. What I mean by that, is every day you wake up and go to sleep with the same event playing over and over in your mind. Nothing seems to help, and then just when you think everything is okay, you find yourself crying and having your own pity party because this painful memory just will not go away.

Every time your perpetrator walks in your proximity, you start having cold sweat, your heart starts growing cold all over again. The only thing missing is the fiery furnace that has not yet come out of your nose. Why do I keep feeling this way, you ask yourself, when will I be free from this nightmare and be able to love and trust again? You wonder, when will you be able to even function properly ever again and have your emotions back to normality? I just want to be free, but I can't let myself out of this cage. I have no strength. Someone needs to come and rescue me. I see the key, but I don't want to reach for it because that means I have to step out again and I know they are just waiting out there to hurt me again. So, you just stay in your own private painful cage silently screaming only to never be heard.

Why me, why me, why me? You keep crying that you are the victim and that they should be the ones paying for all the injustice that they have inflicted on you. How dare they move on with their lives and here I am, God's Chosen vessel, left here to deal with the aftermath of this unfair circumstance. As you have read in the previous chapters, I too have had my share of heartaches. However, there are times you will not have any words to articulate the amount of pain that you are experiencing, not to anyone, not even to yourself. I know it feels like you are not going to make it, you can't go through another day watching everyone around you live what they call the wonderful life, while you struggle in your own sorrowful circumstance. The pain is so deep and unbearable that you begin to ask yourself, is this how the lives of God's Chosen people are designed and orchestrated to be? So many questions and it looks as if I'm getting little or no answers at all. I would like to extend the hope and comfort to you dear Chosen one which is found in Hebrews 4:15 KJV, "For we have not a high priest which cannot be touched with the feeling of our infirmities; but was in all points tempted like as we are, yet without sin."

You see you have an elder brother named Jesus and He wants to let you know there is nothing you have gone through that He cannot identify with you. He simply invites you to bring all your cares and your burdens to Him, even the unforgiving heart that won't allow you to walk in total forgiveness, so you can be free and liberated.

Nothing that happened to you was your fault. You were merely a victim of life circumstances, the decisions of others, and or the unhealthy decisions you made. Regardless of what category you fall under you don't have to remain a victim. You can triumph from a victim into a victor and learn how to release the hurt to your Heavenly Father, who is able to bear all the burdens that life, and others, or even yourself may have thrown at you. You really can't carry any of it by yourself and still have the desire to have a heart that has room enough to forgive yourself and those who are offended. It is only when you decide to reach out and make amends that you can walk in total freedom and victory from those who have caused you much pain. I have learned the art of forgiveness resides on a one-way street, you see because no matter how much you try to apologize or humble yourself and ask the individual that has hurt you for forgiveness, you may find that they want to keep you in a state if victimization because they desire to see you stay in a cycle filled with constant sickening bondage with them.

You have to make the wise decision that you will not allow them to have that kind of control over you. State your peace and choose to move forward. I would like to share a revelation given to me by the Holy Spirit, our greatest comforter and counselor. I was going through a season where I was being attack via the worst injustice filled with all sorts of malicious hatred, jealousy, backstabbing hypocrisy, false rumors they were advancing to me back to back, the experiencing was such cruel and disgusting behaviors that was being display by those who I considered my loved ones, as well as from those in the house of God, and also from total strangers whom I didn't even know.

Now you know when you are dealing with warfare, the enemy is trying to get you to walk in the spirit of offense. I got so frustrated and upset and I went to cry out to my Heavenly Father, like His servant David did in Psalms 21:9 KJV, "Thou shalt make them as a fiery oven in the time of thine anger: the Lord shall swallow them up in his wrath, and the fire shall devour them." This scripture written by God's Chosen servant David, resonated well with me. I thought it was only fair, I said to my Heavenly Father, that He dealt with these people in the same manner as the scripture above.

I could not understand what I had done wrong. I have always tried my best to walk in peace with everyone, as much as possible. When it was not possible, I would dust the dirt off my feet and move forward. After crying out to God for understanding, and telling him they should pay a great and terrible price for treating me with such evil and malice hearts, The Holy Spirit gently whispered to my spirit to go to the Book of Ephesians 6:12 KJV, "For we wrestle not against Flesh and blood, but against principalities, against powers, against the rulers of the darkness of this world, against spiritual wickedness in high places." The Holy Spirit began to show me the above scripture and gently explained to me that the attacks were not coming from the individuals themselves, it was the enemy of your soul who wanted to steal your joy and peace and He was using them to get you off course. He then went on to explain to me that I should not get offended by the people, I should use my spiritual eyes to discern the spirits that are in operation in those individuals because to the Holy Spirit they were still souls who needed to be saved.

However, the evil and manipulating spirit is what I needed to remind me daily to put on my whole armor to properly fight and respond to those attacks as stated in Ephesians 6:10-18 KJV, "Finally, my brethren, be strong in the Lord, and in the power of his might. Put on the whole armor of God that ye may be able to stand against the wiles of the devil. For we wrestle not against Flesh and blood, but against principalities, against powers, against the rulers of the darkness of this world, against spiritual wickedness in high places. Wherefore take unto you the whole armor of God that ye may be able to withstand in the evil day, and having done all, to stand. Stand therefore, having your loins girt about with truth, and having on the breastplate of righteousness; and your feet shod with the preparation of the gospel of peace; Above all, taking the shield of faith, wherewith ye shall be able to quench all the fiery darts of the wicked. And take the helmet of salvation, and the sword of the Spirit, which is the word of God: Praying always with all prayer and supplication in the Spirit and watching thereunto with all perseverance and supplication for all saints."

Dear Chosen one, it is God's will for you to walk in the fullness of life that He has designed for you to live in. Do not allow others, not even yourself or life circumstances keep you in the unforgiving bondage a minute longer. Yes, you can love again, live again, smile again, and feel again. Remember Chosen one, no other individual can hold you back from experiencing life's greatest joy and peace, only you can. Let me bring to your remembrance the step toward a pure heart of forgiveness can simply be done by forgiving yourself and your offenders. *Let us proceed...*

CHAPTER-9
THE RESTORATION TRUTH

Now, what is that all about? The restoration process is the part in your Chosen Journey when you come to the realization that all of the brokenness that you've experienced was designed for a purpose, and that very purpose was to make sure that you would be restored back to God's original state which God intended for you before the foundation of creation. In Joel 2:25 KJV, "And I will restore to you the years that the locust hath eaten, the cankerworm, and the caterpillar, and the palmerworm, my great army which I sent among you." To be restored in Webster's Dictionary states: "to give back, to return, to put or bring back into existence or use to bring back into a former or original state, renew, to put again in possession of something." Once again, we see that these two definitions are not much different. The Bible declares, God knows the end from the beginning, so why does being a Chosen vessel require such drastic measures to see all of God's promises and tangible manifestations come to pass in your life? Whenever God wants to do anything, He will start from the ground and work His way up. God will make sure that the foundation in which He wants to build your life is sturdy and unmovable. Hence, the reason that being Chosen will require a refining and a rebuilding experience.

The enemy of your soul came with one purpose and that is to make sure you never reach the Chosen path that your Heavenly Father has created and designed just for you. Why is that you may ask? Well, let see if you were created like Lucifer to live and dwell and the presence of God, and you being one of God's ArchAngels and your primary role was to bring God all the glory and honor due to Him from His beloved children. However, you decide as Lucifer did, that he wanted some of that praise, glory and honor for himself. How do you think that will affect us as God's children? If you responded, not well at all, then you are right. That is exactly what happened, when Lucifer made the conscious choice that He wanted to share in a glory that did not belong to him, all of us as God's children became affected with his selfish and prideful ambition. Lucifer and a third of the angels were evicted from heaven and sent down to earth, where he chooses today to rule and reign. Although, in God's word nothing has changed in Psalms 24:1 KJV "The earth is the Lord's, and the fullness thereof; the world, and they that dwell therein." The enemy thinks he is in charge, but a famous saying of the saints today is "The devil is a liar and yes the father of all lies"

Therefore, here we are living and walking out this faithful walk daily and oftentimes feeling like, Lord, what I am doing, or better yet Lord what are you doing? Do you see all that I am going through? Standing and confessing your words daily but nothing is changing. What am I Chosen for again? Lord, What Now? What is this journey all about again, please Lord remind me? Well, you have asked all the right questions and you are heading exactly toward the plan, purpose, and destiny regarding all of God's sovereign will for your life. We know that by now, as we live this Christian life that our Heavenly Father is a God of decency and order. Therefore, let us examine this restoration process and all the promises that God wants for all His Chosen sons and daughters to experience. All I know is that in order for God to declare to His Chosen ones that their time of total and complete restoration has come, there must have been chaos and turmoil, confusion and obscurity in your life in one way or another, which would provoke God himself to make such bold statement promising to bring you to complete restoration in every area of your life. I can look at my life, as I had to walk in my own personal Chosen journey and also knowing that God had made several promises for my life that had not yet come to pass. It really seemed like the opposite of His promises, prophecies, and declaration of the goodness of the Lord were happening in my life. It was more like I was experiencing the worst of those proclamations.

I could not understand and so I cried out, "Lord I am doing all that I know to do, but I am tired and weary. I have people speaking against me and making their own judgments over what I felt was such a pitiful and painful situation which I was already living in. I am serving you, praising you; I am in covenant with you, giving my tithes and my offerings, in my heart I know that I am doing all that I know to do. But yet the promise of restoration seems so very far away from me." The root word to restore is "rest" which means to repose, sleep; free from activity or labor; a state of motionlessness or inactivity; a place of resting or lodging; peace of mind; something to use for support. However, I found myself having no rest or a place to lay my head, going from home to home, being rejected by those who should have loved me, as you have read in the previous chapters in this book. The provision of the Lord seems like nothing short of begging, or merely existing. I could relate to Lazarus the beggar in the bible, Luke 1:20-21 KJV, "At his gate was laid a beggar named Lazarus, covered with sores, and longing to eat what fell from the rich man's table. Even the dogs came and licked his sores." This passage speaks of the dogs being the only ones to bring comfort to his wounds, not his friends or his family. Where were those, who should have been there in his hour of greatest need? Lazarus, the beggar, was experiencing what you and I will, in some shape or form, experience also doing our Chosen Journey. Lazarus' story is similar to the wilderness process of what the life of God's Chosen vessels will often look like during that period of time.

This was a glimpse of the Chosen life of this man of God. We are not exempt. Like our Lord and Savior, Jesus, desperately asked of God to let him not go on this Chosen journey and destined assignment, we too will have some things, in our Chosen Journey, that we will have to walk through, live through, cry through, and press through. This Chosen and peculiar journey will most certainly be much too much for you to bear all by yourself. In other words, not everything will make sense to you while you are on your Chosen journey. I remember doing this difficult and unbearable time that my only heart's cry to God was at that time Lord where you are? God, what did I do to deserve such treatment, such abandonment? I was in a place of great loneliness and depression, a miserable feeling that says that my whole being was here when really the truth be told that my body was present but my mind was nowhere to be found. My desire to live and survive daily was next to nothing. I had no zeal, I was broken, wounded, shattered, discombobulated, smiling on the outside, and severely broken on the inside from so many of life's traumatic blows. I was experiencing everything all at once at that very moment, all the pains in which I discussed in depth in the previous chapters of this book were overtaking me. I was truly on the hanging on edge for dear life from the little hope I could muster up as I was also plunging head first on the verge of a nervous breakdown. I became numb. I simply existed by going day to day with the normal routine of life feeling absolutely nothing. There were days I did not want to get out of bed. A do-not-disturb sign was all I could put up in my mental mind and pray that somehow others would see this sign and no one would ask me any questions, because I had absolutely no words or explanation. I wanted everyone to keep going on as they already had been. Not seeing me, not hearing me, and not even acknowledging my pain, my brokenness nor my deep and sorrowful heart's cry for comfort or help. How dare they were enjoying their lives, while I was depleted and barely getting through day by day. Where was God's fairness and restoration? There was nothing to live for. Zilch, I concluded in my infinite mind. All men are liars, I wanted to scream at the top of my voice and tell God that I wanted to desperately put him in that same category as well. But something deep inside of me would not let me go there. I honestly just wanted out, out, out, out. I thought and felt that I could not take any more of this mundane, providential life, when God told me He had more for me in abundance than I could ever have imagined or fathom. I say all this to you so that you do not become delusional God's Chosen vessels learn from my experience dear chosen one. If you are a new babe in Christ or have been one of God's longtime generals, or even if you are just a seasonal church goer. You will face some tough roads and dilemmas that will cause you to question your very faith, or existence, especially if you are a believer in Jesus Christ. If you feel a pull from the Holy Spirit to come into God's marvelous Kingdom, know that the Chosen journey and your 'yes' to the call and purpose of God for your life, will not be one with a road map but a total and complete surrender to the obedience and guidance to the Holy Spirit.

This Chosen journey will most certainly have you question your entire faith in God many times over. This Chosen Journey that you are on can and will only be done in God's ability and never by your own might, or power. You will find yourself asking many of these same questions below, and many more, several times along your Chosen journey and in your walk with God. Questions such as; God, where are all your promises? God, where are you? God, why are you doing this to me? God, do you not care about what I am going through? God, can you hear me? The question 'why?'At that time was all my heart could muster at certain times and seasons of my Chosen journey. I was hurting beyond despair and God was nowhere to be found. Everything I was experiencing was so very far from God's version of what true rest or restoration was. I recall being taught and reading in God's word even as a young child that God would give me rest if I cast everything to Him, but either I did not want to remember or maybe no one mentioned to me during this time that God has his own timing to bring all of his promises to pass. I remember being at my breaking point when I would cry out to the Lord, and He gave me a scripture in His word to let me know that He still has a plan and a purpose for my life. He emphasized on the truth, that I was not forgotten and that my situation and circumstance was not my final destination. I know right now you may find yourself in your own Chosen journey and you will wonder what is going on? Where are the promises of the Lord? Why are they not coming to pass in my life right now? Somebody please help me, this is not the life of a believer, that I signed up for.

If you are reading this book, and feel that you are at this stage of your life where you have believed God for something you have been talking about for so long; or there is something you have been desiring from God; or there is something you have been asking God for; or there is something you have been proclaiming; or there is something you have been feeling The Holy Spirit conviction about. I would kindly say congratulations to you, for you are now entering and experiencing your Chosen process toward God's full restoration in your life. Let me be clear, the Bible plainly tells us in Isaiah 55:8-9 KJV, "My thoughts are not your thoughts, nor are your ways My ways, ways, and My thoughts than your thoughts." This scripture shall bring joy and excitement in your heart to let you know that you have not missed God, nor your Chosen destiny and purpose with the Lord. God is a master orchestrator, and He has already made known your end from the beginning. The crooked road that you feel you are traveling on has already been made straight by your Heavenly Father, all you have to do is keep walking, trusting, believing and know that God is not a man that He should lie nor the Son of Man that He should repent.

Our God is the God of restoration, and it is not just anyone's restoration, but 'YOUR' own personal restoration; not just your neighbors' restoration, but 'YOUR' own personal restoration; not just your pastors restoration; but 'YOUR' your own personal restoration; not just the man and woman of the Bibles restoration; but 'YOUR' your own personal restoration. Hear me and hear me well, God your "Abba" is indeed the God who will bring to pass every promise and prophetic word that He has ever spoken in your life shall come forth. When will my time of full restoration be, you ask? How much longer do I have to wait? The word of God declares that we are able to decree a thing and see it established. I come under the authority that I have in Christ Jesus my Lord and Savior; that your hour of restoration of all things, in every area in your life, is here in the 'NOW' not tomorrow; not later but in your now Chosen divine purpose for the full and tangible manifestation of all things to be restored and be visible in the realm of the spirit and in the natural realm also to become, real and evident, in every facet of your life. Fret not dear Chosen one, continue to believe your Heavenly Father's word over your life is nothing but the truth and it is being revealed even now as you feel His very presence consuming you with his warmth and compassion as He leads you to the finish line, and all the while God is holding your hands as you walk side by side to your final and blessed Chosen destination together. The time will surely come when you will look back and be able to see that it was all a divine set up by God and God alone who has brought you into His mighty and spacious place of all things being made new over every area of your life.

125

The Bible declares in Psalms 23: 5 KJV, "Thou preparest a table before me in the presence of mine enemies: thou anointest my head with oil; my cup runneth over." Therefore, have you had a lot to cry over the last couple of midnight seasons in your life. Have you believed God until there was nothing else you could do but just stand? Have you praised until your voice could no longer utter a word? Have you decree a thing until you have nothing left in you to decree? Have you shared your heart with those you trusted until they were tired of hearing about your situation? Have you? Have you? Have you? I can ask you these 'have you' questions until you and I are blue in the face. However, the only one that can hear our heart's cry for the promise of the restoration He has promised us, is our Heavenly Father. He knows the length of time and season that we must walk through as His Chosen vessel. However, if like His servant David, you can say that my tears have become my meat day and night, while everyone is asking, where is your God? I can safely say to you that you are indeed in good company and also a partner and member of the God's Chosen club. The word of the Lord to you is that He will restore, not just in some things, but all things in regards to you spiritually, financially, emotionally, or physically, psychologically and more and yes God will restore all things concerning your life completely. Hear the word of the Lord and hear it well. God's total and complete restoration comes not in some things but in everything. Everything, and again I say to you—everything.

The word of God states in Ecclesiastes 3:1 KJV, "There is a time for everything, and a season for every activity under heaven." Yes, you have had to walk through a difficult time and season of lack, where there was no rest for you, where everyone and everything seems to have been taken away from you. Please understand God was not punishing you, He was simply laying a new foundation and stripping you of the old foundation to renew and bring you forward to all of His promises and prophetic words into your life. You will look back, and like God's servant Joseph, and say it was good that I was afflicted. And yes, even like our fellow servant in the Lord, Joseph, has declared "you meant it for evil, but God used my affliction, my circumstances, my obedience and willingness to submit to His Holy Spirit and Authority to save much people alive." God birthed this book in me while I was still in my tremendously painful Chosen journey, waiting for my season and time of restoration and all of my numerous promises from the Lord. I have also gone through many of those heart breaks, which you are going through even as you are reading this book from the Lord. The apostle Peter says in 1 Peter 4:12-13 KJV, "Beloved, think it not strange concerning the fiery trial which is to try you, as though some strange thing happened unto you: But rejoice, inasmuch as ye are partakers of Christ's sufferings; that, when his glory shall be revealed, ye may be glad also with exceeding joy."

You may be at the very place right now, where your heart has been broken while doing the work of the Lord. Even with all your faithfulness and due diligence, you have had things, people, loved ones and life come after you with a fury and vengeance like never before to make you miss your Chosen purpose, concerning God's call and destiny for your life. The enemy of your soul whispering, and sometimes even shouting, at you that you will not make it, that your time of complete restoration will never come. Well, let me be the first to congratulate you as you are holding this book and it is because God wants to also walk with you into your own restoration journey as He did with me, and as a result you are holding this book of God's faithfulness to me as I have allowed Him to restore me to His original intentions and divine purpose over my life. For you see the enemy said that I had miss my time and season of restoration, well you are reading this anointed and appointed divine book because of God's faithfulness for it is God who has brought me to the fullness of all of His restoration for my life, and I now know it is not only for my own personal time and season of restoration, but it is also so that I can encourage you and let you know that you too are a Chosen vessel of the Most High, and that you have not missed your God's perfect timing and destiny for your life as you are now entering into your own season of rest and restoration, regarding God's plans, purpose and destiny for your life. You are very well on your way, and again I extend a heartfelt congratulations to you God's Chosen and blessed vessels because you decided to trust God and not quit on your Chosen journey. Chosen, Now What? The end of this procession has come to a halt; Please dear Chosen one "Give yourself permission" to proceed toward your own God's Chosen journey of restoration in all things concerning your life; and remember that on this journey of spiritual self-discovery, God has already orchestrated and calculated each and every single step of His restoration journey for your life. Trust and believe that He has already figured out every single step you will ever take as you walk through God's path towards your complete wholeness and total restoration. **All the best, God's Chosen One**.

CHAPTER 10
FINAL WORD OF LEGACY POEM

I will Tell the World that I am a devoted Christian. I am not ashamed Jesus Christ name to represent. I will tell the world how Jesus Christ saved me, how He gave me a brand knew life. And what Jesus Christ has done for me, He will do it for do for you. Let's, tell the world that you are a devoted Christian, be not ashamed Jesus Christ powerful name to represent. Let's, tell the world that you are a Christian and take Jesus Christ with you everywhere.

CHAPTER 11
SYNOPSIS

Chosen "Now What." Are you new to your spiritual journey or have been patiently waiting around for your purpose and destiny to come knocking at your door? Have you done all that you know to do, but you are still waiting on the sidelines of the familiar face of rejection, loneliness, hopelessness, and discouragement? Allow me to take you into my own personal journey of my self-discovery of purpose and destiny. If you would not mind taking my hand and come walk along with me on this journey. This spiritual mandate will help you to obtain the keys of the Kingdom, to help you move from the sidelines of being a spectator and become a part of the winning team called life. You are called to live your best-Chosen life, because the Captain of the team did not make a mistake when He chose you to play in the biggest game of this season of your life. Playing safe or hard will not be the only components that help you stay and win this chosen game. It will be your tenacious and valiant spirit, along with all the biggest cloud of witnesses and the people God has called to personally lead, who will watch you step by step as you gain your greatest victory in the biggest game of your LIFE. Remember you are Chosen to win. Now, let's embark on this journey together where you will discover the very tools you will need to WIN. *Let's Go!*

www.ingramcontent.com/pod-product-compliance
Lightning Source LLC
Chambersburg PA
CBHW051318120626
46547CB00015B/2297